teaching stories

about the author

Judy Logan has taught middle school at inner city public schools in San Francisco for twenty-eight years. For twenty of those years, she was a teacher in the school where she was once a student, and where her mother, aunts, uncles, sister, and cousin once attended. From her second floor window she could see the hospital where she was born, her grandmother's home where her mother first brought her as an infant, the back of the house she grew up in, and the roof of the house she lives in now.

In contrast to this rootedness, she has traveled extensively and has completed courses in Women's Studies in Kenya, India, Israel, and Hawaii. She has been a mentor teacher in San Francisco for the last nine years, working on multicultural and gender inclusive curriculum. She consults to the National SEED (Seeking Educational Equity and Diversity) Program and the Minnesota SEED Program.

She now teaches a mixed grade middle school class at San Francisco Community School, a small K–8, teacher-run, alternative public school.

teaching stories

judy logan

MINNESOTA INCLUSIVENESS PROGRAM
saint paul

TEACHING STORIES is a publication of the Minnesota Inclusiveness Program, which is funded by the St. Paul Companies.

Published 1993. First Edition.

Production Coordinator: Cathy L. Nelson
Book and cover design: Claudia Smelser

Library of Congress Number: 93-91529
ISBN: 0-9636822-0-2

Printed in the United States of America
10 9 8 7 6 5 4 3 2

to Peggy McIntosh

contents

preface

IN 1986 MY friend, Ellen Boneparth, wrote me from Israel that she was planning a Women's Studies Institute at the Hebrew University in Jerusalem, and that she would like me to attend. I had met Ellen when I participated in the Aegean Women's Studies Institute in Greece three years before, and we have been friends ever since. I told her that I could not afford the fees for her program and the airfare to Israel, and she replied that I could attend the program in exchange for some free rent in my home when she returned to San Francisco in the Fall to teach at San Jose State. This offer was too good to pass up. So I spent the summer in Israel, and in September Ellen was living in my spare room.

One day she told me that she was attending a party that evening, and that she was nervous because her seventh grade teacher was going to be there. "This woman changed my life," she said. "She was the first feminist teacher I had ever had. I'm so nervous that she won't remember me, or that I won't have the opportunity to tell her what a positive impact she had on me."

Being a sixth, seventh, and eighth grade teacher myself, I loved hearing this story. The next day I asked Ellen how it went. "Oh, it was perfect," she said. "I walked into the room and Peggy said, 'Ellen Boneparth, how nice to see you,' and I had a chance to really talk to her."

Two summers later I was standing in line waiting to register for "A Women's Place Is in . . .the Curriculum," a workshop sponsored by the National Women's History Project. There was a large crowd clustered around the reception desk in a Santa Rosa motel and only one person to help us with room registration, so I began chatting with the pleasant-looking woman standing next to me. We grumbled a little at the long wait, and somehow our conversation turned to the fact that we had both been in Nairobi, Kenya, for the UN Decade for Women Forum the year before.

"Did you go as an individual, or did you go as part of a group?" she asked.

"I went with the International Women's Studies Institute," I said.

"Then you must know Ellen Boneparth. I think she directed that program."

"Yes, Ellen is a good friend of mine," I reply.

"She was one of my students. I was her seventh-grade teacher."

I am delighted. "Then I know who you are! You must be Peggy McIntosh! Ellen has told me so much about you," I say. "I am a teacher myself and I loved hearing about your teaching."

Peggy and I are in conversation for the rest of the four-day conference. In fact, I love our talks so much that I stay an extra night in Santa Rosa just so that we could have one more dinner conversation together. I had been teaching middle school for twenty years when I met Peggy, and I had been working on gender-inclusive, multicultural curriculum for many years, but I had never read her 1983 article on "Interactive Phases of Curricular Re-Vision," which explains, among other things, various phases of awareness teachers are likely to go through as they try to include womens' studies into school and college curriculum.

Since then, I have had a chart in my classroom which I title "Judy Logan's Oversimplification of Peggy McIntosh's Interactive Phases of Curriculum Re-Vision." Here is a brief synopsis: Phase One: There are no women in curriculum and nobody notices that they are not there; Phase Two: People begin to notice that they are not there, so they begin to look around for women who act enough like famous men to be significant enough to put into history (sort of like "add a woman and stir"); Phase Three: The problem phase. Historians *want* to put a lot of women into history, but they can't find any except protesters. Women are angry and focus on issues: sexism, racism, classism, and so forth. Everybody seems angry; Phase Four: History, or curriculum, is *redefined* to put women at the center. Now women don't have to behave in a certain way to get into history. Everything they do *is* history; Phase Five: History is redefined to put us all at the center.

Peggy's Phase Theory applies not just to women, and not just to history. It can be applied to any group of under-represented people, and it applies across the curriculum. I also love the parts of her essay that talk about changing the climate of the classroom from a "win lest you lose" mentality to one in which we are all concerned about mending and caring for the fabric of our daily lives.

As Peggy tells me about her theories, I tell her about my classroom. I tell her stories of my students, of the joyous/heartbreaking, funny/sad, boisterous/quiet, scary/satisfying daily realities of my teaching life. Her theories validate what I have been trying to do in my classroom for a long time. My stories flesh out her article with examples.

By the time our four days together are up, we are good friends. Although it will be two years before I see her again, Peggy and her work have a profound influence on me. Eventually I become part of her National SEED

(Seeking Educational Equity and Diversity) Project, conducting faculty development seminars in my own school district in San Francisco, and participating in summer workshops co-led by her and the SEED Project Co-Director Emily Style, in Colorado, Minnesota, New Jersey, and California. The national and international network of SEED teachers that is now a part of my life can be traced to that moment that I stood in line and grumbled to a stranger about the long wait to register.

This year I am on sabbatical leave. It is my twenty-fifth year of teaching. One of my projects this year has been to write my teaching stories. Some of these stories I told to Peggy while we were in conversation in Santa Rosa. Some of them have happened since then. It is my hope that these stories will generate ideas on how to put students at the center of curriculum and how to create a classroom environment that is not based on a "win lest you lose" mentality.

It is my belief that all students benefit from an inclusive curriculum, not just females, or African Americans, or Native Americans, or Asian Americans or Hispanic Americans. I believe . . . But, wait, I think these stories will show what I believe.

*   *   *   *

Thank you to Peggy McIntosh and to the Center for Research on Women at Wellesley College for sponsoring this sabbatical project. Peggy's encouragement, inspiration, assistance, patience, and validation were invaluable. Thank you to the American Association of University Women for the Eleanor Roosevelt Grant. This financial cushion provided me with the time and security necessary for reflection. Thank you to Cathy Nelson, Brenda Collins, Nancy Letts, Janice Koch, Emily Style, Dena Randolph and my SEED sisters and brothers for giving me the courage to speak in my own voice. Thank you to Gail Dent for providing me with the comforts of her home to use as a work space. Thank you to my colleagues Kathie Edeli and Frank Foreman, whose dedication to children and commitment to education are a daily inspiration to me. Thank you to everyone who read these stories and made me feel like a "real" writer.

Special thanks to the Minnesota Inclusiveness Program for publishing this book, to Claudia Smelser for designing and producing the book and cover, and to M.D. Barrera for her careful proofreading.

Most of all, thank you to my students, who never stop teaching me, and to their parents, who entrust me with the lives of their children.

foreword

USUALLY, IT IS "not done" to write the foreword to a book dedicated to oneself. But in the spirit of Judy Logan's own teaching, which so often raises the questions of "Why not?" and "What if . . . ?" I took up the unusual honor she offered. I see it as a chance to accept a gift and pass the gift along. Much of my own life history has this sequence, and perhaps much of our happier schooling in thought, emotion, and spirituality has this pattern of receiving and recognizing gifts, and passing those gifts along.

It takes my breath away to open a book on education and find it so peopled. In most educators' writing, I can't see a student for miles around. The mapped City of Educational Abstraction is not offering any hot lunches. I hear the sounds of cranes and trucks and jackhammers demolishing old structures for the further expansion of the city. But what happened to all the people?

Teaching Stories is richly peopled with students, parents, and teachers, living vividly in the moments of their lives. Over Judy Logan's shoulder you can see and hear them. She is the participating narrator. The classrooms and hallways never quiet down. The city beckons for another field trip. I can imagine why Logan's sixth, seventh, and eighth graders have wanted to read these chapters. These stories are theirs. At the same time, they are the stories of an extraordinarily imaginative, hard-working, and enabling teacher.

Most educational theorists refer to other educational theorists. In *Teaching Stories*, Judy Logan derives educational theory from many years of immersion in the intense, exciting classes which she creates. Her theories are often grounded in and deftly presented in the language of the classroom. Using the students' own language, she writes of her balancing of the "have to's" and the "get to's"—by which she means the things students are required to do as against the ones in which they may follow their inclinations. She captures a whole paradigm shift in her dialogue with her five-year-old niece, who says, "Teachers know everything." "No. Teachers know some things. Nobody knows everything . . . " And later, as "The Story of Two Quilts" so tellingly illustrates, "Students have their own stories."

Most writing about education, together with most teaching, evades the matters which most frighten and confuse adults, which we are unable to "master." Judy Logan allows for discussion of these life matters as they arise in students' lives. Therefore, *Teaching Stories* has many startling, frank, comic, poignant, and disturbing scenes. They result from one teacher's day-in-and-day-out commitment to what philosopher Jane Martin terms the three C's, needed beyond the three R's, in education: Care, Concern, and Connection.

I wish that Judy Logan had been the teacher of our own children because she herself has such a gift for recognizing the intelligence, heart, and soul of a young person, and teaching to that with precision and split-second sensitivity. She teaches without condescension or evasion and with commitment to the growth and development of each student in her care. This results in the growth and development of parents as well, as many parents in these teaching stories testify.

Students have many economic, social, and emotional uncertainties which Judy Logan helps them to acknowledge and think through, as they negotiate their complex lives. The collaborating teachers of her school are shown making effective networks of support for students. In times of crisis, these teachers may need to be committed to keeping students alive. On a daily basis, the book shows teaching which respects the students' experiences of love, hate, cruelty, fear, jealousy, hope, pleasure, excitement, intuition, and above all, creative imagination and intelligence.

Surviving the curriculum guide, as Logan puts it, is another kind of life challenge for teachers. Our students rarely want to come to school because of the content of the formal curriculum. They come to see their friends. They may come because it is better than home or the street. But Judy Logan makes the curriculum interesting, varied, textured, so that it provides for each child, in the words of Emily Style, windows into the experience of others, and mirrors of the student's own reality and validity. The students feel co-ownership. The stories testify to prodigious learning.

Some educational theorists fear, or claim to fear, that pedagogical innovation and greater curricular inclusiveness will undermine U.S. educational standards. The "standards" now supposedly in effect have produced abysmally poor results, especially with regard to students' basic skills of reading, writing, use of numbers, critical thinking, and becoming decent citizens. I believe that Judy Logan's students do outstanding work in all of these areas, not despite her innovative teaching, but because of it.

For example, in anonymous judging year after year, Judy Logan's students sweep the prizes in the essay contest which hundreds of students from all over the city enter. And year after year they impress the students and teachers in the high schools and colleges they go on to attend. Year after year they have impressed me, as I have met them or heard from them in spontaneous letters. It is not very usual for a young person to attribute the discovery of his or her distinctive style of intelligence to an enabling and empowering school or teacher. Judy Logan's students do so. They have a distinctive honesty, integrity, and sense of play which they (and I) attribute in part to her recognition of their lives as persons in their own right, full of real and potential life.

The success stories recounted in this book tie in with and validate most of the major educational reforms in the United States today. Many educators are exhausted by the quantity of school reforms, seeing each as dealing with a new and different problem area, and therefore burdening already overworked educators with ever more "shoulds" and "oughts." I believe that most of the recent education reforms have a generalized coherence which those who developed them (often in competition with each other) didn't see, or didn't admit to seeing. A single chapter in *Teaching Stories* is likely to bring to mind, illustrate, or illuminate, several reforms at once.

Among these are team teaching, collaborative learning, faculty development, attentiveness to learning styles, school restructuring, peer counseling, writing across the disciplines, gender equity, race equity, cooperative learning, alternative assessment, literature-based instruction, multicultural curricula, school/community programming, interdisciplinary study, family life education, global studies, peace studies, hands-on math and science, conflict resolution, parent involvement, values education, and the role of teacher-as-researcher.

In listing these movements and initiatives separately, I depart from the immediacy of *Teaching Stories,* which I see as an important book in late 20th century U.S. educational history precisely because of its syntheses embedded/embodied in stories. The separated, competing reforms are the isolated buildings of the City of Educational Abstraction. *Teaching Stories* brings schooling to life organically, as in Maya Angelou's land of river, rock, and tree, where people and provisioning for our actual journeys of living and dying are at the center of education.

I have said that Judy Logan's teaching implicitly asks of old prohibitions "Why not?" and "What if . . . ?" We know that for many students school is boring, irritating, insulting, or frightening. Teachers who wish to change school environments, however, may be obstructed at every step. Many teachers have it in them to teach in some respects as Logan does. They should not have to work so very hard against school norms to do inventive, healing work in education. School structures need to give talented teachers space to do what they do and share what they know. Like students, teachers need places they *want* to be in, places which respect their imaginations and knowledge.

Teaching Stories testifies to some brilliant ways in which we might teach to students' and teachers' actual human needs and interests. In these stories you can see it happening: the students, the class, the aliveness, the commitment to education as growth and development for all. Judy Logan is in the picture, but she does not block our view of the students. One editor, in rejecting the manuscript of *Teaching Stories,* wrote that this book "is not about teaching as most of us understand it." Exactly, which is why "education as we understand it" is in so much trouble.

Year after year, Judy Logan's former students return to visit her. As *Teaching Stories* testifies, they realize how powerfully she worked to enable them to do what they learned to do. In grades six, seven, and eight, however, what they knew most clearly was that they were co-creating the education they were receiving. In retrospect, they value the educator who divined and entered into serious conversation with their own beings. All of this is made clear in the book in language which is candid, poignant, engaging, and alive. Perhaps Logan's style of writing will do for all readers what she does for students—help us to trust ourselves, our voices, our experiences, our own stories in the stream of time.

Peggy McIntosh, Wellesley College Center for Research on Women
Wellesley, Massachusetts
April 1993

Some of the stories in this book took place three years ago, others span my teaching career to its very beginning in 1966. These stories are true, but all student and parent names have been changed, as have some details of stories.

A word about tenses. I often start a story in the past tense, because it happened a long time ago, but I switch to the present tense to give the reader a sense of immediacy. This is deliberate and I hope it will not offend too many English teachers.

the story of two quilts

NOW THAT MY five-year-old niece has entered kindergarten, we have an on-going philosophical discussion about education. "Teachers know Everything!" she says, often and adamantly. "Since you are a teacher, you know Everything!"

"No," I say, "teachers know Some Things. Nobody knows Everything."

"Yes," she says stubbornly, "TEACHERS know EVERYTHING."

"But there are some things you know that your teacher doesn't know."

"Like what?"

"Like what it feels like to be Molly's big sister, to be your Mommy and Daddy's older daughter, to be Gary's good friend, to be my five-year-old niece."

But so far she hasn't bought it. She insists teachers know everything.

In my twenty-five years of teaching middle school, one of my goals has been for my classroom to be a blend of some of the things I know, and some of the things my students know.

The quilt experiences serve as an example. Two years ago someone made an anonymous donation to our school. One day I read in the daily bulletin that up to $200 was available to teachers of academic classes for art projects relating to their curriculum. I began thinking about how I could use art to further enhance our studies of women.

This was late in the semester, and we had already done extensive autobiographies, written essays for the NOW essay contest, and researched African American men and women's lives for Black History Month, so the students felt somewhat connected to the lives of women in their own families as well as women in science, politics, art, social reform, music, sports, literature, journalism, space exploration, law, civil rights, education, humor, etc.

I wrote a proposal to the administration explaining my idea for the quilt project and was granted the money, and we began class discussions on how to proceed. I put a big piece of butcher paper on the blackboard, with the word "Inclusive" at the top, and asked the students to develop a list of what we needed to keep in mind in order to make our quilt truly inclusive. Hands popped up, and students volunteered categories first. We should have women in medicine, sports, law, civil rights—the list grew.

What else? How else can we make this quilt inclusive? What else do we know about diversity? Hands popped up again. We should have Native American women. Hispanic American women, European American women, African American women, Asian American women, Lesbian women, straight women—again, our list grew. Then, we put the two lists aside, taped to the wall, so we could still see them. We began to brainstorm a list of individual women who were possibilities for quilt squares. Before beginning to choose which woman to honor on each student's square, we created a very long list of possibilities. This list included people like Nancy Reagan, Jackie Kennedy, and Martha Washington, who did not end up on the final quilt itself, because thay did not fit any categories in our first two lists. The students decided that they didn't want to have a lot of president's wives on the quilt, and ended up honoring Eleanor Roosevelt and Abigail Adams, who fit other slots on the first list, such as Social Reformer.

When we finished brainstorming these three lists, we noticed that we didn't have anyone who was a Filipina American, and there is a large Filipino community in our school, so we sent two students downstairs to the Filipino Bilingual class to explain our project, and to ask them for suggestions on Filipina women we could honor on our quilt. These students returned to class and told us the story of Vicky Draves. We learned that she was the first American woman to win the gold medal in the diving category at the Olympics. She still lives in San Francisco in the South of Market neighborhood, and the Filipino community is lobbying to get a city gymnasium named in her honor. She used to practice diving as a child by taking the mattress from her sister's bottom bunk on the bed, putting it on the floor, and diving off the top bunk (students were of course warned not to try this, as they might end up in the hospital instead of in the Olympics).

Melissa and Mariko decided they wanted to work together on Vicky Draves' patch. Other students knew immediately who they wanted to do. Some had a hard time choosing between several possibilities. When they discussed this with me individually, we would look at our first two lists, and consider which choice would make our quilt most inclusive. By this time in the semester, the class was committed to including women of color as a high priority.

But Alicia wandered around for two or three days, looking at reference books, and becoming gloomier and gloomier. "What is it, Alicia?" I asked.

"I can't find anybody that I want to do. When I think of someone, somebody else has already got her. I don't like this assignment. I don't want to do it."

"Who are the women in your life that you really care about?"

Pause. "Damara Bennett, my ballet teacher."

"Well, why don't you do a patch honoring your ballet teacher?"

She immediately brightens up. "Can I do that?"

"Yes, you can do that. You won't be able to read any books or articles on her, but you can do primary research through interviews, phone calls, or letters, but that shouldn't be a problem for you, since I know you go to ballet lessons every day, and see her frequently."

Alicia's whole attitude towards this assignment changes. The next day she brings in her pink toe shoes to use as models as she fabric-paints her square. The other students admire the shoes, and she gets to talk about her dancing. My other ballerina/student decides to do a patch on Isadora Duncan.

Before we begin the quilt, the students bring up the question of grading and evaluation. I have told them that I envision the quilt to be a work of art that will inspire and teach other people about the lives of women in America. I see the quilt hanging in the classroom, in other schools, in libraries, post offices, in other public places, and I see it accompanied by a book, with the women honored listed in alphabetical order, and with a statement by each artist telling who that woman is, and why he/she chose to honor her on this quilt. So the assignment has two parts: the quilt square, and the written piece for the book.

This causes great concern. "But some of us have never sewn anything before, and some people might be really great sewers. It's not fair to grade us on our first attempt at something."

"True. I want you to feel comfortable taking some artistic risks here. So, what shall we do?" I ask.

"Well, we're already really good writers, but we don't know yet if we're any good at sewing. Maybe we should just be graded on the written part."

(I take a moment to silently do a little dance with myself because they are identifying themselves as "really good writers," which they would not have done at the beginning of the year.)

"That isn't fair to the ones who are better artists than writers," other students protest. After some discussion, we decide that they will all do the best work that they can on both the quilt square and the written piece, and they can each choose later which part they would prefer to be graded on. This feels fair to everyone.

We spend a few days in the library and in the classroom doing research. We talk about symbols, about how to represent a person's values and accomplishments symbolically. Meanwhile, I telephone my friend Ellen in Santa Cruz, who is a fifth grade teacher and an Art mentor teacher for suggestions. My art skills are limited, to say the least. She suggests that I buy some black fabric to frame each square and to frame the quilt itself. "It will kind of tie things together," she tells me.

I go to the store and buy lots of unbleached muslin for the squares, some black cotton fabric for the borders, and a large variety of solid and patterned bits of colorful material. I also purchase lots of embroidery thread, needles, and embroidery hoops.

I take the whole class on a field trip, walking four blocks to the Names Project headquarters. The Names Project collects 4 by 6 foot quilt squares made by the family and friends of people who have died of AIDS. The class has just finished our nine-week family life unit, and this is the last trip we are taking to see how our community is responding to the AIDS crisis. Nancy Katz, the education director at the headquarters, meets us outside. She greets us, and takes us inside, past the sewing machines and the people working on them, and asks us to sit on the floor in a circle. She tells us about her job; she explains the history and the meaning of the Names Project. She shows us the shelves and shelves of folded quilt squares. She shows us a video about the Names Quilt in Washington, D.C. After answering student questions, she gives us a poster for our classroom, and since the artist of the poster is in the room, he comes and signs it for us. We look at the quilt squares hanging on display, the symbols on them, the love and care stitched into them. They are inspiring. We tell Nancy about our incipient quilt project, and she is very supportive and enthusiastic. "I will come and help you put it together," she tells us, "and I will loan you some tools that will make measuring and cutting easier." I thank her.

As we are walking back to school, red-headed Deirdre starts walking next to me and measures her steps to mine. I know she has something to say and I wait for it to come. "Can I do her?" she asks, meaning Nancy. "Yes, what a good idea," I reply. "I will give you her phone number, and you can arrange for a time to interview her. I think she would be happy to be on our quilt."

Roberta, Deirdre's best friend, says, "Can I do Deirdre's mother? She's the woman I admire most in the world."

Yes, I say. I believe in saying yes to my students. Sometimes I say no, but I don't say it lightly, and I try to give all my reasons (I never say, "Because I said so," which I have heard other people say). I believe that students have reasons behind their requests, and that it is important for me to learn about them in order to really teach effectively. Usually when I get to a place in the curriculum when I have to say no to a student's request, I have a fair amount of trust built up because of all my yeses, so they are more likely to take risks. But that is another story.

"Can Juan and I work together? We both want to do Julie Croteau, the first woman ever to play on a college male baseball team, and we're not good at sewing, so can we work together?"

Yes.

"Can I do Dian Fossey? Annie already signed up for her, but I REALLY wanted to do her, she's the only person I REALLY want to do. No, I don't want to work WITH Annie, we don't work well together. Can I?"

Yes. (It is interesting to compare these two Dian Fosseys later. The male artist has a big gorilla overpowering the square, no Dian. The female artist has put Dian in the center of the square, with a small gorilla in the background.)

"Ms. Logan, can I take my square home and work on it?" Yes. "Can my mother help me?" Yes. "Ms. Logan, I have made two squares on Isadora Duncan and I don't know which one I like best." "They're both wonderful. Let's put them both on. After all, this is a quilt about being inclusive."

Seventh and eighth graders begin to hear about the quilt. They come in at lunch time. "Can we do a patch too?" Yes. "I have some great fabric at home that I want to use. Can I bring it in?" Yes. "Can I do Cyndi Lauper?" Yes. "Can I sew on buttons, ribbons, sparkles?" Yes. "Can I stuff cotton underneath to make it three dimensional?" Yes. "Can I do Shakespeare's Juliet, even though she's not a real woman?" Yes. "The only thing I really care about is swimming. Can I do someone in swimming?" Yes. (Hence, Esther Williams.) "I want to represent all the women who were here before Columbus 'discovered' this land. Can I do the Forgotten Woman?" YES!

"Ms. Logan," Jessica asks, "Can I do you?" Yes, I would be honored. "I already figured out what I'm going to do—I'm going to put your necklaces on my patch."

Frankie, an eighth grader, asks if she can do herself as Future Woman. What a good idea, I reply, and give her a blank patch. The next day, she brings in the completed square, along with a poem for the book:

> Faces
> From the past
> Fade
> Exist only
> In memory
> Faces
> from the present
> are in the moment
> But only for the moment
> But
> Faces
> Of the future
> Are forever
> Because future
> is infinite
> So many possibilites

Frankie is a talented actress. She wins city-wide contests for visual arts and for her essays in the annual NOW contest. She sings with the school choir. She excels in math and science. To say she is a student with many possibilities is to use understatement.

I bring my sewing machine, my iron and my ironing board to class. I buy a set of lower- and upper-case letter stamps and a black ink pad. We decide to put each woman's name at the bottom of our patch to add continuity to the quilt. We begin to set up stations in the classroom—this desk for stamping your patch, this area for measuring and cutting, this area for ironing, this area to learn embroidery stitches, this area for fabric paints. Students who are experts in each thing sit next to that area to help others.

One of the first things that I notice is that only girls gravitate towards the ironing board, and only boys gravitate towards measuring and cutting. Every other station has both boys and girls working together. I think about what to do about this. Finally, I decide to ask Frank, my male colleague and friend, to drop by class and to casually start to help us by ironing. I am hoping that in modeling this behavior, he will give the boys permission to try it. The next day, he does just this. He comes in, admires all the activity, and asks the girls if he can help by ironing for awhile. I go and help with the measuring and cutting. Immediately, several boys gravitate to the ironing board and ask him if they can help. While they are ironing, I go over and visit. "Do you iron at home?" I ask them. "Oh, yes, I do all the ironing at home," one of them says. "I do napkins and tee shirts," another one reports. They all iron at home.

"You're very good at it," I tell them. And I make a mental note. It wasn't that they COULDN'T do it. It wasn't even that they didn't WANT to do it, since they were certainly eager enough to help once Frank was in charge. They just needed a male role model to give them permission to do a "girl's job" in the public arena of the classroom.

I give some thought as to who I want to honor on my patch. I decide to honor Brenda Collins, who is also named Eagle Woman. She is a member of the Bird Clan of the Cherokee Nation. She is a medicine woman, the first woman in her clan to get a Ph.D., and a teacher of psychology at Santa Rosa Junior College. She is a friend and a mentor. I have heard her speak several times, and I remember her saying that to be an educated Indian woman is like having a foot in each of two canoes in rapid waters—always balancing two cultures. I decide to put two canoes and rapid water on her patch, with an eagle's wing by one canoe, and her doctoral degree by the other canoe. I read that the Cherokee Nation believes that the people came from the stars, from the Seven Pleiades, so I buy seven glass stars to sew in the corner, and, because I myself love the moon, I buy a glass moon to put on as well.

I am having a good time cutting out my canoes, stitching them onto my patch, stamping Brenda's name at the bottom of the square, painting the eagle's wing, writing my piece for the book. Several computers have been set around the room so that students can type their written pieces onto discs when they are ready.

A parent brings in some of her own fabric paints and a book of designs that can be ironed on fabric for embroidery outlines. She stays to show us how to use the materials.

As the patches are finished, we use masking tape to fix them to the blackboard, making new rows when needed. We discuss how many rows to have, how many patches to a row.

John is having a hard time with Georgia O'Keefe. He has a good image in his mind, but he can't get it to work on the square. I send him to work with Suzanne, our AV clerk, who I know is a good artist, a kind and patient person. She herself has volunteered to do a patch on Joan Baez.

A young woman who works as a part-time aide in the special education department, and who is an art student part time, takes home a blank muslin square. She returns it with an incredibly realistic air-brushed portrait of Billie Holliday.

One student, Thomas, has been struggling with cancer since he was six months old. He has had radiation, chemotherapy, and surgery, and he has lost an eye. This sixth grade year is the first time he has had a whole year in school since third grade. Writing his autobiography was very traumatic for him, and involved building a lot of trust in class, and he did end up claiming his illness as a part of his life in his autobiography. He even included pictures of himself in the hospital, bald and frail after chemotherapy. Thomas chooses to write about a family friend who is a film maker, Felicia Lowe. In his written piece, he tells about Felicia's first film, "China, Land of My Father." Then Thomas writes, "Two years later her second child was born. She wanted to make another film but when they discovered that her daughter had leukemia, she could not continue. It took two years for the chemotherapy to destroy the dangerous form of cancer. When her daughter was well, Felicia went to Angel Island to make her second film." Thomas continues Felicia's story in terms of her film career. But it is the caretaking of her daughter that is the real story here. Thomas, too, has stitched his own story onto this quilt.

The class responds positively each time a finished square is taped onto the board. The exceptionally beautiful ones make the whole quilt look better. The less than beautiful ones look nicer when taped up with the others. Nobody says, "Mine is better than yours." We are each a part of a whole.

It is time to measure and cut the black fabric to sew the rows of patches together. Not everyone is finished with his or her patch, but we begin with the rows that are complete. We are doing fine until my sewing machine breaks. I call parents. The next day, Linda Clayton and Carol Larson arrive with their portable sewing machines. They stay for several days. They sew while students iron open their seams, work on the computers, help others.

I take time out now and then to notice and appreciate what is going on. The energy in the room is calm and relaxed, but focused and productive. Students are self-directed and supportive of one another.

Jesse is doing a patch on his grandmother, who took him and his Dad to New Zealand over the Christmas break to visit her birthplace, a sheep farm. It was a "Roots" journey for them. Jesse decides to put a sheep, a kiwi, the airplane that transported them to New Zealand, and a rose (which is his grandmother's birthday month flower), onto his square. He also decides to learn how to embroider the entire patch, since his grandmother loves to embroider. It is the first time he has used needle and thread, and he does a remarkably good job. Jesse is a great kid; he is outgoing, sometimes disruptive, and not always cooperative. (For example, when we rode the streetcar to an ice skating field trip, Jesse got in trouble for riding on the BACK of the trolley, through the TUNNEL, no less, and he has been known to throw spitballs in the theater.) To watch him quietly absorbed in his embroidery is a thrill.

Shoshannah had lost her great-grandmother, Bubby, in February. She writes about this loss for her quilt piece, and for her square she decides to embroider her family tree, with Bubby as the trunk. Her mother, her aunts and uncles, her cousins, her brother and herself are all branches and twigs, and she embroiders their family names. But most of her time is spent painstakingly stitching different shades of brown into the thick, strong trunk. She sews her grief and her love for her great-grandmother into her patch. She works on it in class and at home, but it is the last to be added to the rows on the blackboard, and at that she still doesn't have enough time to finish. She ends up having to color in the small unstitched part of the trunk with brown fabric paint.

The student I have been most worried about decides to do Esther Williams. This child's story unfolded slowly this year, and took many hours of counseling and support services from social workers, but we were finally able to legally get her out of an abusive home. Looking at her patch on Esther Williams in a typical synchronized swimming pose—her head pointing towards the bottom of the pool, her legs pointing out of the water towards the sky, I notice that the swimmer has no arms. This could be because it is difficult to depict the sculling action of a swimmer's arms that make this position possible. It could also be her artistic rendition of her emotional state. I also notice that she has depicted a colorful, happy mermaid, perched on the edge of a wave, looking over this upside-down swimmer.

Another student, who has also had some traumatic experiences this year, has decided to do Dorothy from *The Wizard of Oz*. But early in the project she comes to me and asks, "Can I do my other teacher, Starhawk, instead?" Yes, I reply. It seems Starhawk has done some healing work with her this year. I give her one of my glass bead stars to sew onto her patch. I rationalize that we can usually only see six of the Seven Pleiades, anyway.

One of my Hispanic male students, Alberto Martinez, does a lovely job embroidering a generic square honoring all Mothers.

Garrett, whose writing always contains many references to blood and gore and scary horror stories, does a generic quilt square honoring women doctors. But the doctor he depicts has a blood-splattered white gown, a huge needle dripping blood in one hand, a bloody scalpel in the other. On the examining table huddles a small, scared child, who looks a lot like him.

My eighth grade student, who we have seen through a suicide attempt (she slit her wrists in school one morning), sews a square honoring Cyndi Lauper, and writes about how much Cyndi's music has helped her. Her best friend, Rebecca, does her patch on Juliet, the only heroine from literature on our quilt: a thirteen-year-old who kills herself.

Our personal histories and our class experiences are stitched into this quilt.

Another eighth grader wanted to do her square on Anne of Green Gables. She even talked one of her red-headed friends into cutting several inches of her hair so that she can give Anne real braids. But, unfortunately, she doesn't get around to sewing a patch. The idea stays just an idea, and her friend's hair is shorter for nothing.

It is now just a few days before the end of the term, in June. Our squares are framed in black, and we have a border for the edges. Each step we take transforms the quilt. Linda takes the quilt home and spends an evening sewing in the cotton batting, and sewing the sheet on for backing. The next day we spread the quilt out on several tables and take turns knotting through the front, batting, and backing. Meanwhile, we are finishing up typing our pieces into the computer.

I bring the discs with the written pieces to my friend, Craig Johnson, who donates his time printing them professionally. I run off copies so that each student has a copy of the book, and I make one special copy that will hang next to the quilt. The day before the end of the term, we take the quilt outside to photograph it. During lunch, I take the film to a nearby processing place and order enough copies so that on the last day of school I can give each student a photo of the entire quilt, and a close-up photo of his or her own patch, as well as a copy of our quilt book.

I buy two copies of *Hearts and Hands*, a book about women and quilts, to give to Linda and Carol. I pass the books around the room so the students can write their own personal thank yous on the blank pages at the front and back of the book. "Without you," one boy writes, "our quilt would just be scraps of fabric."

Someone says, "Don't you wish we could each take it home and sleep under it, and write down our dreams?"

The finished quilt is colorful and diverse. No two patches are the same. I have provided the outline, the framework for the assignment, but each participant has created something unique.

I spend some time internally going over why this assignment worked, using my favorite frameworks as guidelines.

I think about the Bay Area Writing Process. Yes, we did the whole process for the book part—pre-writing, writing for fluency, response, writing for form, and evaluation. We stressed process more than product.

I think about Peggy McIntosh's "Interactive Phases of Curricular Revision." I notice that we have Phase Two patches, like those of Abigail Adams, Elizabeth Blackwell, Amelia Earhart, Sojourner Truth, Harriet Tubman, Alice Walker, and Ida B. Wells. Some can be thought of as Phase Three patches, such as the ones for Ann Simonton, the woman who did street theater in Santa Cruz to protest the beauty pageants there and who dressed herself in raw steaks, saying women were not just "pieces of meat"; and Lolita Lebron, the Puerto Rican woman who spent many years in jail for bursting into Congress shooting and shouting for Puerto Rican independence; and Forgotten Woman, representing the many Native American women left out of history books. And we have many Phase Four patches, like Nancy Katz; Deirdre's mother; Jesse's grandmother; Alicia's ballet teacher; the classroom teacher (me); generic patches for mothers, doctors, and astronauts; and my personal favorite, Future Woman.

I think about Gregoric's learning styles. There has been a place in this assignment for those who function best in the concrete world. There has been a place for those who function best in the abstract world. Some students worked sequentially, some students worked randomly. There has been room for both.

I notice that we have used Bloom's cognitive skills—knowledge, comprehension, application, synthesis, evaluation. There has been a lot of encouragement in the creative process, and the affective area has involved listening, cooperating, teaching, sharing, encouraging. The process of making the quilt has brought us closer together as a class. Even those of us who made less than perfect patches delight in the finished product.

I think about my own guidelines on inclusive curriculum. As much as possible, if I control the content, I try to let students control the form. If I control the form, I try to let students control the content. I think of this as the "have tos" and the "get tos." As in yes, you "have to" do a quilt patch, yes, you "have to" do a woman, BUT you "get to" choose the woman you want to honor on this quilt, and you "get to" do your patch any way you want to.

I ask myself, did this lesson empower my students, or was it a "power over" experience for them?

I ask myself, was this separated knowing, or was it connected knowing?

Was it a doubting game, or a believing game?

Was it about care and connection, or was it about winning and losing?

Did it get across the idea that history is all of us?

I think about Emily Style's metaphor of curriculum as window and mirror. Emily says that all students should be able to see themselves mirrored in the content of curriculum, in terms of gender, ethnicity, race, and class, and students also should be able to look through the windows of curriculum into the stories of people who are "other" to them. And I suddenly see this quilt as a collection of windows and mirrors, in their small black frames, some patches being windows, others mirrors, some both. We see ourselves in the feminine humanity of this quilt.

The quilt travels with me when I do summer workshops in Colorado, Minnesota, New Jersey and California. Other teachers respond to it favorably. Peggy McIntosh says she likes quilts because, among other things, "there is no head patch." This is true; it has felt like a non-hierarchical assignment. When we taped the patches to the wall, they just fit without any preconceived ordering. Nobody fought about whose patch was first, or last.

I also think about how good curriculum is like a Haiku, that form of Japanese poetry which follows a particular form, but which is constructed in such a way as to allow the audience to bring their own experiences into the construction of meaning. It leaves a corner open for the reader to enter in. Not only did each student bring her or his own experiences into the quilt (Shoshannah's family tree, Frankie's vision of herself in the future, Garrett's bloody doctor), but each observer of the quilt is encouraged to participate (What woman would you choose to put on your patch? Who is missing from this quilt? Who on this quilt do you already know? Who is a stranger to you?). I think all curriculum should be like that. Yes, there needs to be a form, an outline, clear expectations, but there also needs to be that corner open for the students' stories to enter in.

My friend Sara takes our quilt to Esprit, a well-known clothing manufacturer in San Francisco that collects and displays quilts, and their professional photographer takes better pictures of it, and gives me the negatives. But mostly, the quilt hangs in my classroom, after a short display in the glass case of the school library.

The next year, when the new sixth grade class comes into my room and sees the quilt, they say, "Will we get to do a quilt too?"

Oh yes, I say, wondering whether I will have the time and energy for it at the end of the year, wondering where I will get the money.

But a parent of a former student, Alan, has received a grant to do art in the schools. He volunteers to teach the unit. HE will buy the fabric, HE will plan the borders, HE will sew the batting and the backing together, HE will supervise the work in class. I can be one of the students, just making my own patch, writing my own piece. I am very grateful. I don't have to spend my own money, or spend my lunch periods at the fabric store, or use my math skills to figure out how many inches each patch will be, or how many patches to a row.

Alan and I work out our time schedules. I have the students two periods in a row, so he decides to come in two days a week, and work for a two hour stretch, so we won't have to spend a lot of time putting materials out, then putting them away again. The iron and the ironing board return to school.

On the alternate days when Alan is not there, the students and I work on how to choose a person to honor on the quilt, how to do research on that person's life, and how to write a piece for the book that will hang next to the quilt.

Hanako, who was so seriously ill this year that she required hospitalization and many painful blood transfusions, chooses to do Gilda Radner, the *Saturday Night Live* comedienne who had just died of cancer. Leslie decides to do Lucille Ball, who had also just died.

Emma does a patch on "Teacher Love," her nickname for her pre-school teacher, Sylvia Bradley.

Ethan does a patch on Jane Goodall, Janet chooses Zora Neale Hurston, Johannes does Helen Keller, and Tabashi does Annie Sullivan. Lucy chooses Louisa May Alcott, Raoul writes about Sarah Winnemucca, Akiko does her patch on Martha Graham. Craig writes about Clara Foltz, the first woman lawyer in California. Lance does a generic quilt square on Rosie the Riveter, honoring all working women. Christa McAuliffe, the teacher in space, and Margaret Sanger, birth control pioneer, are included. This year, the idea that history is all of us has really sunk in, and eighteen of the thirty-five squares honor the students' mothers, grandmothers, aunts or godmothers.

The riveting square that looks like Lana Turner, with her blonde hair pulled over one eye, is really Molly's story about Lana Smith, her relative who was a pioneer farmhand, and who lost her eye to cancer after it was hit by a rock.

Matt writes about his great-grandmother. Andy, Gabriella, and Brian honor their grandmothers; Stella, Susan, Ralph, Samantha, Julia, Robbie, Melanie and Jason choose to do their mothers. Simon writes about his aunt, Nancy. Rose writes about her mother's best friend, Louise Jones, Rose's "godmother and heroine," who is a composer. One day, Rose's mother stops by school, and I bring her up to my room to see the quilt in progress. We both stand there admiring it. She gets teary and says how wonderful it is to see her best friend included. She tells me the story of one of Louise's compositions called "Emily's Nap." Louise had adopted a young daughter, Emily, who was hyperactive, and who never slept during the day. This composition was for the drums, and was a noisy rendition of the reality of Emily's non-existent "naptime."

When students finish their writing for the book, I sign them into the computer lab for the final printing.

The process of quilt-making is different this time. Alan cuts out all of the squares for us. He talks to us about the skills he will teach us—how to draw portraits so that the eyes are in the middle of the egg-shaped face, how to cut out rubber stamps backwards so that the letters appear correctly on the patch, how to mix fabric paints to get proper flesh tones, how to paint backgrounds in colors that enhance your portrait, how to frame your square in contrasting colors to deepen the effect. He talks to us about symbols, and he shows us the square of his grandmother that he has painted for us as an example.

We learn a lot of techniques that we didn't know before.

I decide to do Faye Wattleton, the now former president of Planned Parenthood. I use the photograph of her with her daughter in the book, *I Dream a World*. Each child brings in a photograph of the woman he or she is making for the quilt. We look at these photographs carefully as we make our preliminary drawings. Alan does a stunning second square on Ella Fitzgerald.

We begin our drawings on tracing paper, then trace the outlines of our drawing in black felt pens, then tape our muslin squares over the black outlined drawings on the windows, so that the dark lines show through. When we have traced the basic shapes onto the fabric, we are ready to go to the art room and begin mixing the paints for the skin tones. We use each others' skin for examples, and I love watching us asking our Asian American, European American, or African American friends to put their forearms near our patch while we struggle to mix the exact shade. Jason agrees to be my model for Faye Wattleton's skin.

Alan is incredibly well-organized, patient, knowledgeable, and talented. He has a vision of how this quilt will look, and what skills he wants to teach us, and I notice a subtle thing happening. The students begin to ask questions. "I am painting my grandmother, and I would like to bring in some of her earrings to sew on the quilt."

No, but you may paint the earrings on.

"Can I bring in some special buttons to put on her dress?"

No, but you may paint the buttons on.

"Can I do a profile of my person?"

No, in the interests of continuity, all of our portraits will be full face.

"Can I stuff cotton in mine to make it puff out?"

No.

In order to make his vision (and it is a lovely one) work, Alan needs to say no to the students' visions.

There are a lot of "have tos," and not enough "get tos."

Something happens to students when we say no to them. There is a subtle but real disconnection. A resignation. A giving up. Sometimes, resentment. I watch it happen.

The resulting quilt is dazzling. It doesn't sag or gap like our first year quilt. Instead of having black borders, each square is framed in a contrasting color. Students have painted in the entire square, so the overall effect is denser. But when I look at each individual square and begin to talk about the stories behind each patch, I often can't remember which child did which square. They look too much alike. I worry about what might have been sacrificed in order to make this vision work.

This Diversity Quilt is less diverse in its form, but it is more Phase Four in its content. Having last year's quilt as an example helped a lot. ("Can I really do my MOTHER?!")

Again, I photograph the quilt and order forty copies. I photograph each square so each child will go home with a picture of the quilt and a close-up picture of his/her square, along with a copy of the quilt book. I plan an evening to display the quilt, give out the pictures, and say good-bye, since I am leaving for a one-year sabbatical. We invite all of the parents, as well as the aunts, grandmothers, godmothers, teachers, and mothers who are honored on the quilt. I bring two cakes that say "Congratulations Seventh Graders," since they have all just passed into the next grade, and students also bring cakes and cookies. We move the tables aside, set out chairs in rows for our guests, put out coffee, tea, napkins, and paper plates.

The quilt is completed, hanging at the front of the room. Alan has even bought a bamboo pole for it to hang from. Each student takes a turn coming to the front of the room, pointing out his or her patch, and telling the story of the person he or she is honoring. It is a treat for me to watch this affect the audience. Aunts smile, grandmothers get teary, everybody feels good. Only one mother feels that her daughter chose to do her because "she was too lazy to do research on anyone else."

When the two quilts hang side by side, they are each beautiful. The second quilt shows that each student went through the process of learning portraiture techniques and also something about color theory and mixing and using fabric paints. Each square is a face. By controlling both the form and the content of the lesson (what we are doing and how we are doing it), there has been less room for experimentation on the part of the students and because of this their own stories have not surfaced.

So the first one is still my favorite. When my five-year-old niece is old enough to understand, I'll use it as an example to further explain to her that teachers don't know everything. Students have their own stories.

stealing stories

A FEW DAYS after I had attended a theater performance with a large group of seventh and eighth graders, a parent telephoned. "Judy," she said, "this phone call is strictly confidential. Please don't let on that I've called you, but something has happened that I think you should know about."

She then proceeded to tell me that her daughter and three of her good friends, each of whom was an excellent, well-behaved student, had gone to Woolworth's Five and Ten Cent store on the way home from the theater, and they were caught stealing something—I think it was a lipstick. All four of them were taken to the manager's office, lectured, threatened with the police, and kept there until their parents could come and pick them up. This parent then tells me that the girls are really humiliated and ashamed, and they are very worried that I will find out what happened and think less of them. They are remorseful, nervous, and anxious.

This is a great time to read my Stealing Stories to the class. These Stealing Stories evolved over the years almost by accident, but have been so successful in building trust in the classroom that I now highly recommend them to other middle school teachers. Basically, they are four stories about teenagers who steal something. But the role of the wise adult figure in each story is wonderfully unusual. Instead of becoming angry, instead of fostering shame or humiliation in the child, the adult uses the stealing incident to foster self-esteem and to develop wiser decision-making skills.

It is my experience that not all students have perfect parents, and it is my experience that middle school years are rife with crises, so I use these stories as a way to foster a wise parent within the child herself/himself, so that if a parent, or parent figure, uses a shame-based approach during a crisis, the child will have an internal alternative voice to listen to.

Am I saying that the act of stealing by an adolescent is an opportunity to foster self-esteem and wisdom? Yes, I am. It is in making mistakes that we are most vulnerable, and it is in this vulnerablility that we are most likely to listen and grow. The flip side of this, of course, is that it is also during these vulnerable times that adults can do the most damage to children.

Hence the stealing stories, wherein I offer my students four adults who understand this vulnerability and who use it as an opportunity for transformation. The first story is from the novel *Mama's Bank Account*, by Kathryn Forbes. In Chapter Eleven, "Mama and Big Business," Katrin is working in Schiller's Drugstore for three hours every afternoon while Mr. Schiller goes home for a hot lunch. Her friend Carmelita comes to the store to keep her company, and before long, they take to stealing a Hoeffler's Centennial candy bar every day, enjoying it, and throwing the box and wrapper up onto a shelf over the front door, to hide the evidence of their theft. They feel guilty, they keep promising themselves they will stop, but they keep doing it. One day, a man comes in to change the window dressing above the store, and discovers all these empty Centennial boxes and throws them down onto the first floor. Katrin is horrified, and before she has a chance to say anything, Mrs. Schiller yells at her and lectures her, calling her a thief. Katrin rushes home to Mama in tears, and Mama offers her understanding:

> "This is important, my Katrin. Perhaps I cannot explain it so well, but you must not ever feel here—" she touched me—"in your heart, that you are what you said. A - a thief. A bad girl."
> "But, Mama, I did take them—and Mrs. Schiller said—"
> "Katrin, believe me, you are not a thief. You are a good girl."
> I shook my head. "You have been foolish, yes, you have done wrong. But no great wrong. You are still so young—so greedy for sweets, as all young things are."
> "Mama, you just don't understand!"
> "But I do, that is why—" And Mama's laugh rang out suddenly, richly.

Mama continues by telling Katrin about the time that she was living with Aunt Jenny, and Papa was courting her. Each Friday night Jenny would make cookies, or a cake. Once she made a beautiful cake that was piled high with white frosting. Mama was young, she, too, had a sweet tooth. She kept sneaking into the pantry and tasting the frosting, until finally there was no frosting left on the cake. Katrin laughs with Mama at this story. "What happened?" she asks, and Mama tells her that Aunt Jenny served the bald cake to Papa and told him what had happened.

"And what did Papa do?" Katrin asks. Mama smiled a secret smile. "He married me," she said, "anyhow."

Earlier in the story, Katrin says about stealing the candy, "But, Mama, whenever I think of it, oh Mama, I am so ashamed."

"Is good to be ashamed," Mama replies. "That makes it sure you will not do such a thing again. But cannot you see, Katrin, that with the shame and the sorrow there must also be the saving laughter?"

When I discovered how much my students loved this story, I looked for another one, and discovered William Saroyan's "The Parsley Garden." This story takes place during the Depression, in Fresno, California. It is about a young boy named Al Condraj who steals a hammer at the five and dime, is caught, and is made to stand in the manager's office for a long time before he is allowed to go home:

> The first thing he did when he was free was laugh, but he knew he had been humiliated and he was deeply ashamed. It was not in his nature to take things that did not belong to him. He hated the young man who had caught him and he hated the manager of the store who had made him stand in silence in the office so long. He hadn't liked it at all when the young man had said he ought to hit him over the head with the hammer... Of course he HAD stolen the hammer and he had been caught, but it seemed to him he oughtn't to have been so humiliated.
>
> After he had walked three blocks he decided he didn't want to go home just yet, so he turned around and started walking back to town. He almost believed he meant to go back and say something to the young man who had caught him. And then he wasn't sure he didn't mean to go back and steal the hammer again, and this time NOT get caught. As long as he had been made to feel like a thief anyway, the least he ought to get out of it was the hammer.

Al lives alone with his mother, who does seasonal work in a packing house. When he goes home he tells his mother everything that has happened. "I don't want you to steal," his mother said in broken English. "Here is ten cents. You go back to that man and you give him this money and you bring it home, that hammer."

"No," Al Condraj said. "I won't take your money for something I don't really need."

Katrin's mother tells her a story, Al's mother offers him the price of the hammer. Each parent cherishes the child's self-esteem and trusts the humiliation of the experience itself to teach the lesson. Neither condones stealing, but neither punishes her child. On his own, Al returns to the store and gets a job shelving goods. His work is so good that the manager offers him a full-time job at a dollar a day, paying him a dollar for his first day's work. But Al takes only the hammer:

> "I left the dollar on Mr. Clemmer's desk," Al Condraj said, "and I told them both I didn't want the job."
>
> "Why you say that?" his mother said. "Dollar a day for eleven-year-old boy good money. Why you not take the job?"
>
> "Because I hate both of them," the boy said. "I would never work for people like that. I just looked at them and picked up my hammer and walked out."

Students love this story, so I offer them another. "Thank you, Ma'am," by Langston Hughes, is the story of a young boy who tries to steal the purse of Mrs. Luella Bates Wahington Jones. This story is particularly fun to read aloud. In it, Mrs. Jones catches the young boy who tries to snatch her pocketbook, hangs on to him, and ends up bringing him home for supper. As the story progresses, we watch the boy's self-esteem grow as Mrs. Luella

Bates Washington Jones offers him her trust along with half her dinner. She discovers that the boy wants ten dollars to buy himself a pair of blue suede shoes, and she not only tells him the story of her own life, but gives him her hard-earned ten dollars before she sends him back onto the street. The boy is so overwhelmed with her kindness and generosity that he cannot get himself to say, "Thank you, Ma'am."

By now we have heard a story about a Norwegian immigrant family, "Mama and Big Business," that takes place in San Francisco, on Castro Street, a few blocks from our school. We have heard a story about an Armenian family, "The Parsley Garden," that takes place in rural California, and we have heard the story about an encounter between an African American woman and child, "Thank You, Ma'am," that takes place on the streets of Harlem. I don't know if these stories had a direct impact on the self-esteem of the girls involved in the Woolworth's incident. They chose never to talk to me about it. I do notice the glances they exchange as they listen to these stories and the discussions following them.

The next story that I read to my students, "Anita's Gift," by Carol McAfee Morgan, is about a Puerto Rican girl in New York City who sees a bucket of roses on the sidewalk. They are unattended, and she takes a bunch, not realizing she is stealing until she gets home. She, her mother and her grandmother, are terrified that the police will arrive at any moment to arrest her. Her big brother brings her back to the place on the sidewalk and helps her return the flowers to the owner, explaining her mistake. The florist is also Puerto Rican, and he responds with kindness. He tells her that he understands her longing for flowers, since their homeland has an abundance of free and colorful flowers. He, too, misses Puerto Rico. He tells her to stop by his store every Saturday night so that he can give her some flowers to take home, as many flowers do not last until Monday anyway. Like the adults in the other stories, he has seen the child's need rather than the child's theft, and he has responded in such a way as to build character rather than to destroy character.

By the time we have listened to and discussed these four stories, we are ready to tell and to write stories about our own stealing experiences. I make it clear that in no way do I condone stealing. But we do talk about what we have learned from our own experiences. We also talk about parenting. We discuss how we will respond if our own children are ever caught stealing, or if they tell us about a stealing experience. My experience is that nobody brags about stealing in these discussions, but they do share comfortably.

Sometimes I continue with two more stories—"A Lickin' a Boy Could Be Proud of," by Helen Eustis and "The Streets of Memphis," by Richard Wright. The first story is about a young orphan who is adopted by a childless couple that own a store. The boy is left to watch the store for a certain period every day, and, like Katrin, gives in to temptation and steals candy. It is the "lickin'" that his new Dad gives him when he is caught that convinces him that they really love him and intend to keep him. This story offers us the opportunity to discuss relationships between love and parental discipline, and to question whether violence in any form is ever approriate. In "The Streets of Memphis," a young boy is given a note and some money by his distraught mother who has just moved north after being abandoned by her husband, and he is told to go to the store for some groceries. Some neighborhood boys beat him up and steal his money. When he returns home his mother gives him another note, more money, and a big stick, and tells him he cannot come back home without the groceries. She forces him to deal with the toughness of the streets. This is a harsh story, and offers many writing opportunities, such as: tell this story from the mother's point of view; write a story about the same neighborhood three months later; or tell the story from a gang member's point of view. Students have strong feelings about the violence on these streets.

From there we can proceed to comparing and contrasting the stealing experiences and the adult responses to these experiences. These stories have presented us with cross-cultural themes, and in each we have found wisdom and kindness, and an opportunity to explore and share our own stories.

gendered journeys

IN ORDER TO keep teaching about gender from falling into the males versus females trap, I believe it is important to begin by letting students focus on their own attitudes, ideas and feelings. Students need to realize their own habits of stereotyping before they can understand them in the larger society. Like attitudes about race and class, attitudes about gender are sometimes invisible, and we can't analyze them or begin to change them unless we make them visible.

The following lesson is one I've used for several years now to bring matters of sex and gender into focus. First, I ask students to clear their desks except for a pen or pencil and a piece of blank paper. Then, I ask them to put their heads down and close their eyes. "Today I will be taking you on a journey back through time. This is not a real journey, it is a journey of the imagination. First, step out of your body and see yourself at your desk with your head down. Now, travel back through time until you are in the fifth grade. See yourself in your elementary school classroom. What are you wearing? Who is your teacher? What are you doing? See yourself at home. What does your room look like? Who are your friends?

"Now, travel back through time until you are in the third grade. See yourself in your third grade classroom. What are you doing? What are you wearing? What do you care about? Who are your friends? What do you do after school? What does your room look like?

"Travel again to the first grade. Notice everything around you. You are learning to read. What are you reading? What does your room at home look like? What do you like to do with your free time?

"Now see yourself as a kindergartener... see how you are playing, who you are playing with, what you are doing. What do you love to do? What do you hate to do?

"Travel again to when you are four. Some of you may have been in a preschool. Some of you may have been at home. Some of you may have been with a babysitter. What were you like then? Notice things about your space. What toys do you play with? Now you are three... look around. Now you are two... beginning to really talk... now you are one... standing and moving around, learning to walk. Travel back again to being a baby... look around your room, at the people around you, at your toys. Now, travel back some more, and here you are, ready to be born!!!!! Everyone is so excited, so anxious, so happy, waiting for your birth... and here you are!! Only this time, imagine that you are born as the opposite sex. So, if you are a boy, pretend you are born a girl. If you are a girl, pretend that you are born a boy. See yourself as a baby, coming home for the first time. Now, see yourself as a year old, learning to walk and move... as a two-year-old, learning to speak. See yourself at the age of three. What are you wearing, what are you doing? Travel to being four, then five, entering kindergarten. See yourself playing in kindergarten. Now move to first grade... second grade... third grade... See yourself in fifth grade. Notice your friends, see your teacher, see yourself reading, see yourself playing after school. Look at your room at home. Now, come back to school, into room 217. See yourself with your head down on your desk. Come back into your body, and when you are ready, open your eyes and sit up. Without talking to anybody, please write a list of how your life seems different since you have been born as a person of the other sex. No one will see this list but you, so be honest."

This guided fantasy provides great focus. Students are always very quiet and intense during this list writing. While they are writing their lists, I tape two large pieces of butcher paper onto my blackboard, labeling one "MALES," the other "FEMALES." When students feel finished with their lists, I say, "Now I would like to go around the room and have each of you choose one thing from your list to share with the class. If this feels difficult, you have the right to pass. Before we start, I would like to add just one more rule. Girls, the boys might say something about being female that doesn't feel true to us. That's okay, we'll have a chance to tell them how it really is to be female later. Right now, it's important just to listen *so we can begin to understand what they think being female is all about.* And boys, the same is true for you. You may hear us saying things about being male that don't feel true to you. Again, you'll have a chance to set us straight later. For now, *listen carefully, so you can begin to understand what our concepts of being male are.*" This is an important caution. Without it, this exercise can deteriorate into a verbal battle between the sexes.

As students volunteer statements from their lists, I write them under the MALE list if they are male students, under the FEMALE list if they are females. Males say things like, "I'd have to talk on the phone a lot;" "I'd have to have a pink bedroom;" "I'd worry about getting pregnant;" "I'd have to get up earlier in the morning so I'd have time to fix my hair and look nice;" "I wouldn't get to play football;" "I'd have to giggle a lot;" "I'd have to do the dishes," etc. Females say things like, "I'd have to be tough;" "I could sleep later in the morning because I wouldn't care how I looked;" "I could play more sports;" "I could stay out later;" "I wouldn't have to babysit."

Perceptive Ellie grumbles, "I think this is a sexist assignment! There are no differences between the sexes. PASS."

("You may be right," I tell her later, "but lots of people *think* there are differences, and it's important for us to find out what they think.")

Once we have gone around the room, I give students the opportunity to raise their hands and add things from their private lists that they would like to see on our butcher paper list. Usually a third to a half of the class adds more items. When a student adds something that is already on the list, I star it. Sometimes something like the pink bedroom statement gets two or three stars.

When our lists are complete, I go over the statements again, only this time the "Real Gender" has an opportunity to tell whether the statement feel true to them. So, if Johnny has said he would have to have a pink bedroom if he were female, I would say, "Johnny, what color bedroom do you have now?"

"White."

I give him a big smile. "My bedroom is white too!!! Girls, how many of you have a white bedroom?" Several hands go up. "Girls, how many of you do *not* have a pink bedroom?" Most hands go up. "So, Johnny, the good news is that if you were female, you wouldn't have to have a pink bedroom."

The tone of the teacher is important here, because we have all received many messages from our culture about stereotyping and grievance in the gender arena. To keep this exercise from being about winning and losing, the tone of the teacher should be about joyful exploration of our stereotypes for the purpose of altering them when appropriate. It should not be about making anybody feel bad, even if what they say might seem outrageous.

When we have finished going over the lists a second time, checking them against our own experiences, I then pass out an article called, "How Would Your Life Be Different?" (Tavris, 1983) We read this article aloud together. This research was done on children in Colorado, and explored the same questions as our guided fantasy described above. Students said extreme things: "If I were born a girl I'd kill myself," or "If I were born a boy, maybe my Daddy would like me." My students are shocked by what this article says. They immediately try to distance themselves from it: "Oh, well, that was in Colorado. Everyone knows that people in California aren't like that. Especially in San Francisco."

"Oh?" I ask them, "Let's take a look at our own lists, tacked up in the front of our room. Our own lists reflect the same stereotypes along lines of appearance, behavior, etc." Because we began this lesson with our own experiences, students are less able to dismiss the information presented in this article. They can begin to own the problem—that our culture projects clear stereotypes onto people of each sex, and that while there are advantages and disadvantages connected with each projection, the advantages are clearly perceived to be primarily for males, the disadvantages primarily to females. The students then participate in class activities on gender more fully. I notice also that they receive information on gender differently, and begin to perceive that their own gender-filter affects their thinking, feelings, and attitudes.

I believe that this kind of personal introduction to gender-inclusive curriculum is essential. We each need to acknowledge that gender systems are about us, *all* of us, males and females. Gender work is not just about including women in curriculum, although that is an essential part of it. It is about bringing our gender attitudes and experiences and assumptions into focus.

random accounts of connected knowing

I HAD PLANNED a Significant Lesson. (I don't remember now what it was, but I remember that I had put some time and effort into making it interesting, varied, and effective. As Roger Taylor would put it, I was the Sage on the Stage that day.) As I begin to present this lesson, I notice that all of the students are properly attentive and absorbed in what I have to say with the exception of one table at the back of the classroom, where four girls are quietly absorbed in doing something else. I become annoyed. Here I am being Significant in a well-prepared way, and they are not captured.

I move closer to their table, hoping that my proximity will encourage better attention. I notice that they have taken crayons and felt markers off the shelf without my permission, and they are each drawing and writing. I become more annoyed. I give the class a five-minute writing assignment so I can deal with this table and get them back into the fold.

I go and sit down at their table, while they continue to draw and write. "What's going on?" I ask. Anat, in a friendly but intense voice, says, "Remember I told you that my older sister, Chris, died several years ago? I was away in camp when it happened, and she was drowned in a boating accident. Well, today is Chris' birthday, and I'm really missing her a lot. I'm making her some birthday cards and writing her a letter, and after school I'm going to go to the ocean and put these papers in the water."

Her friends at her table say, "And we are making cards and drawings too, to make Anat feel better, even though we didn't know Chris. We're feeling pretty sad with her. Do you think that's okay?"

"Yes," I say.

I give the rest of the class a longer desk assignment, and I pick up the felt markers. "Dear Chris," I write, "I love having your sister, Anat, in my class. I wish I had known you too. Happy Birthday."

I postpone my Significant Lesson until tomorrow, when Anat and her friends can better receive it. I thank whatever spirits were present in my classroom that helped me to set aside my annoyance until I knew what was happening.

Anat's parents divorced after Chris' death. Her father moved to Europe and started a new family, and Anat never met these new brothers. She experienced a lot of loss about this, and finally got enough courage to call her Dad and tell him so. As a seventh grader, she was able to go to Europe and spend a summer with him and her new siblings. (The next year we celebrated a joyous event, when her mother remarried and delivered a baby daughter. Anat was at her side.)

Sitting at the table that day with Anat, making cards for her dead sister, helped me to better appreciate the significance of these events in her life.

*   *   *   *

I am teaching a Greek Mythology class. I order a movie about the Greek deities, but another movie arrives by mistake. This mistake-movie is called "The Living Stone." I have seen it many times. It is a movie about Eskimo life, and the title refers to the practice of carving stone in the long winter-time as elders tell the children about their tribal mythology. The stories are connected to the images they carve, and the mythological figure emerges slowly from the stone as the story unfolds. It is a beautiful film about mythology and culture, but it is only loosely connected to Greek mythology. I decide to show it anyway: It is too late to return it and get the movie I ordered in the first place. As we watch, I notice that the students are absorbed in the movie, but I feel a little guilty that I am deviating from our "real" subject. We don't talk much about the movie afterwards, as the class time is up, so I don't get student feedback.

A few weeks later I am talking to a parent of one of the students in this Greek Mythology class. "Judy," she says, "thank you so much for showing that movie about Eskimo culture. Noah came home that day and told us that he didn't want anything for Christmas this year, except for stone-carving tools. He went immediately into the basement and started looking over some old stones we've had for years, carefully choosing one to carve. He's in the middle of this project now. He has a new-found passion in his life." His mother tells me that he described the whole movie in great detail.

I thank her for telling me this. My mistake-movie has had a huge impact on Noah's life. Some time later he brings his carving into his art class. It is a beautiful piece. Like the pieces in the movie, it is as if this figure were already alive in the stone, waiting for Noah to come along and carefully chip and file away its stone casing. We are amazed that this is Noah's first stonecarving. Sometimes connected knowing happens by accident.

*   *   *   *

Today I run into Alivia's mother on the street. Alivia is a junior in high school now, and she has moved to Monterey to live with her father. Her mother tells me that she is rebellious and very anti-authority. She only goes to school part time, and can't wait to get out. "Since she left middle school, she has had a lot of trouble," Alivia's mother tells me. "Her creative self has never been invited into the classroom since she left Frank's and your class."

I think about Alivia as a sixth grader. I remember how earnest she was, how sad that her only brother had left home to attend college, that her parents had just divorced, and that her mother was now at work when she comes home from school instead of at home. I remember how important her dog, Sasha, was to her. She was very open about being lonely and confused. I remember Alivia with affection, and I think about a particular paper she wrote that led me to continue to assign a writing homework piece about a "Food Mistake." Since Alivia wrote this paper, I have delighted in reading it aloud to students. Since we have all made food mistakes, either in cooking or in eating, I've had some great papers over the years.

When I get home from meeting Alivia's mother, I look for and find Alivia's food paper in one of my piles on the floor. Alivia wrote this piece after our International Holiday Pot Luck Luncheon, where parents and students bring food from their ethnic backgrounds to share on the last day of school before winter break. Alivia's paper, which follows, is called "The Pot Luck."

Friday, December 20th, the last day of school, we had a pot luck lunch. We all brought different things. I brought a Christmas log. For this story, we have to go back to Thursday night at seven p.m. I grabbed the cookbook, looked up desserts, and there it was: Christmas Log, or Gina's Nutroll. It called for 6 eggs, separated, 3/4 cup of sugar, (which looked like it said 3 1/4 cups of sugar), 1 1/4 cups of nuts, 1 tsp. of baking powder, 1 tsp of vanilla, and two cups of whipping cream for the inside. After I read the recipe over, I checked over the ingredients and noticed that we needed whipping cream and nuts, so I called Sasha and put her on a leash. We ran up to the store and bought some whipping cream and nuts.

I ran home with one arm carrying the groceries and one with Sasha pulling and running too fast (especially if you have flip flops on). I got out everything and put it on the table. I got out one big bowl and two little bowls for the eggs. I also got the beater. I separated the eggs and beat up the egg whites till it was real thick and frothy. I then poured in the 3 1/4 cups of sugar (still not knowing it was supposed to be 3/4 cups of sugar). The egg and sugar mixed up make it real glazey looking. So then I put it aside so I could mix up the egg yoke which I was supposed to put the sugar in.

I called my Mom to the kitchen and she told me I did it wrong and I was supposed to put the sugar in the egg yoke. So we put in all the other ingredients and tried to bake it but when we took it out of the oven it must have grown 4 inches tall! So we put it in the garbage.

Then we had to start all over. So I called Sasha and put her leash on. By then it was almost 9:00 at night. We walked up there to get eggs and more nuts. We scurried down to the house with me feeling more awful each step I took. Still not knowing about the sugar, I started all over again.

I knew not to put the sugar in the egg whites but in the egg yokes. I separated the eggs all over again. I beat up the egg whites making SURE I didn't put the sugar in. Then I beat the egg yokes and started pouring in the 3 1/4 cups of sugar and the nuts, vanilla, and the baking powder. It then got real hard, I mean hard!

I called my Mom to the kitchen and she read the recipe and saw that the 3 1/4 cups of sugar I put in was really only 3/4 cups. I totally fell apart when she told me. I ran to my room (you really can't run to my room from the kitchen) and sat on my bed sobbing and sobbing. My Mom cleaned the kitchen. I was sad. I asked my Mom to call Ms. Logan and tell her the story. Ms. Logan told us that we didn't have to bring anything. Ms. Logan and my Mom talked for awhile.

When my Mom got off the phone she told me she would make another Christmas Log. So, it was 10:45, and I called Sasha and put her on her leash and we walked up to the store and bought some more nuts. The owners must have thought we were very crazy to get so many bags of nuts! I brought them home with Sasha pulling me down the street thanking me for the walks I took her on. My Mom told me to go to bed and I did.

When I woke up, there in the kitchen was the cake put on the tin ready for the whipping cream to go on it and to be rolled up. My Mom walked in and told me to whip the cream. I said, "No way!!"

So my Mom whipped it up and she drove me to school. I took it to Room 217 where other people were dropping off their dishes. At 11:30 teachers and kids all took their plates and filled them up with delicious things. The pot luck lunch was a great success.

As I re-read this paper I think about Alivia as a sixth grader, still connected to school, comfortable telling her story, able to share her mistakes with us. I remember the big hug she got when she came to my room with that precious dessert. I remember how much the class enjoyed hearing her paper read aloud. I hope that this sixth-grade Alivia is still alive in the angry Alivia who now hates school and can't wait to get out. I worry about what went wrong for her.

*   *   *   *

It is early in the semester, in September. I have planned to introduce the Names paper that day. In this assignment, I read a section from Alex Haley's *Roots*, where he describes how Kunta Kinte got his name. I read a portion of *Ishi, the Last Yahi*, that discusses the power of a name in the Native American community. I tell the story of Rumplestiltskin. I tell the story of my own name. Students then use dictionaries to look up the origins and meanings of their own names, and then write a rough draft in class of everything they know about their own name by answering the following questions: "Who named you?" "What are the meanings of your names?" "Were you named after someone?" "Would you change your name if you could?" "What would you have been called were you born the other sex?" "Were you called anything special when you were still in the womb?" "What are your nicknames and what do they mean?" etc. Students then go home, read their papers to their parents, and ask for further information. The next day in class, when I ask how many students learned something about their naming that they didn't know before, almost all of them raise their hands.

I'm all ready with the materials and the energy to introduce this lesson in a big way, as in the past it has been a popular assignment. But on this day, before I begin, Lance looks up from the back of the room with a very concerned expression on his face. "I just lost my tooth," he mumbles, and I can see that he is on the verge of either crying or smiling. "Congratulations!" I beam at him, and he decides to smile. "Would you like to go rinse your mouth out?"

"Yes." He does so and returns. "How many of you have lost a tooth this year?" I ask, and almost all hands go up. "How many of you have a loose tooth right now?" Some hands go up.

And in the interests of connected knowing, I switch lessons in midstream. Rumplestiltskin can wait. We do the Tooth Fairy lesson instead.

"What does your family do when you lose a tooth?" I ask. Many students eagerly volunteer stories about teeth under pillows turning to money. I tell the story of Latin American cultures that put children's teeth up into the rafters where the rats are, or down into gopher holes, so that the child's new teeth will grow in strong, like the rodents' teeth. I ask my students, "What does it say about our culture that body parts can be exchanged for money?"

(None of the above mentioned lessons are original with me. I learned them all from the Bay Area Writer's Process workshops.)

"Tonight, for homework," I tell them, "describe the Tooth Fairy. Show me, through your writing, what the Tooth Fairy looks like."

"Can we make it into a story?" they ask.

"Yes. But you will be graded on your powers of description," I reply.

I get some fantastic writing the next day, which we read aloud in class. Funny, gruesome, winsome, clever, a whole parade of tooth fairies marches through our class. Some with dental floss hair; some like delicate ballerinas dressed in sparkling, glittering, fantasy clothing; some radical, modern, far-out, and silly; some of them full of Scarey Dentist Ferocity; one with George Washington's wooden false teeth on a string around her neck. Writing these Tooth Fairy stories gives my students permission to hang on to the child in them, as they lose tangible parts of their babyhood and bravely face the unknown territory of adulthood. This assignment says that it is still okay to fantasize, to be silly, to hang on to their rituals.

Not long after the Tooth Fairy lesson, we do our Names papers. These papers are also class favorites. By listening to the stories of each other's names, we learn many things about each other. I staple these papers onto a class bulletin board, and students often go to look at them on their way to sharpen pencils, or when they have a few free minutes. Seventh and eighth graders, who are former sixth-grade students of mine, come in eagerly to see the names papers and spend a lot of time at the bulletin board reading them. I have seen them smile at the newcomers and say, "Nice name paper," as a way of beginning a dialogue, establishing new friendships.

*   *   *   *

It is the last day of school. I'm sitting at my computer in my classroom, typing a final SEED report which is already a few days overdue. My niece, Hannah, is graduating from high school this afternoon, and I'm determined to get this report in the mail before I leave at one o'clock. Several of my students—Sharon, Frankie, Melissa, and Lia—are sitting on the carpeted floor in intense discussion. Sharon is crying. I know these girls and I trust them to work out their conflict fairly. They continue to talk, argue, and cry. I continue to type.

Finally I say, "Is there something I can do to help?"

"Well," they tell me, "we want to cut our afternoon classes and go to the movies. Our parents said it was okay. After all, it is the last day of school and all the eighth graders are gone anyway. But Sharon is not sure she wants to. Well, she wants to go, but she wants us all to stay at school and go to the movies at three o'clock. But the matinee starts at two."

I know these students. They are good students, and I know their parents.

"Well, you have your decision-making list in your binders," I say. "Why don't you get it out and look at it? Use it. " (This list helps them check various steps in decision-making—collecting information, predicting outcomes, checking for outside factors like peer pressure, etc.)

I continue typing away at my report while they do this.

They discuss each item on the checklist and how it is affecting their decision.

Finally Frankie agrees to remain with Sharon at school, and join Lia and Melissa at the movies later. "Does this feel okay now?" I ask Sharon, who has stopped crying. "Yes," she says.

But a moment later Frankie says, "But isn't it also peer pressure if I am doing something that I don't want to do? I don't really want to stay with Sharon, I will do it because she's my friend, but I feel that it's peer pressure."

Sharon breaks into tears again.

"Sharon," I say, "why is it exactly that you don't want to go? Are you against cutting school in principle?"

"No," she says, "I'm just afraid."

"What exactly are you afraid of?"

"I'm afraid the principal will see us leaving and ask us what we are doing. I REALLY want to go with them to the movies, and my parents said it's okay, I'm just afraid."

"What else are you afraid of?"

"Well, the movie is at the El Rey. I'm not sure how to get there."

I think about this. "And you're sure your parents said it was okay?"

"Yes," they assure me.

"I'm going to my niece's graduation in a few minutes. If you want to walk out of the building with me, that should solve one of your problems. And I can drop you off at the Castro Street MUNI station, and you can take the streeetcar through the tunnel to the El Rey Theater. That should solve your second problem."

"Really? Will you do that?"

"Yes."

Sharon is relieved, the other three girls feel that they are no longer abandoning a friend in order to do what they want to do.

We walk down the hall, past the principal, who smiles at us, and leave the building. I am like the Pied Piper, leading children out of school.

A year later, Lia writes in my yearbook, "I will always remember your Shakespeare Class, the India class, Greek Mythology and the Writing Club, but mostly, I will remember you leading children out of the building so they could cut the last day of school."

*　　　*　　　*　　　*

It is the third week of school. After class, Deborah, Anya, and Millie, three of my new sixth graders, stay after class and tell me they want to talk to me. "You are being unfair," they glower at me. "You don't call on us enough—you always call on the other kids. You don't read our papers aloud enough. You don't like us. You are playing favorites." I am upset to hear these complaints. I go back over the last three weeks, mentally, wondering if this is true. It doesn't feel true to me. I wonder what is really going on here. Clearly, these girls are mad at me.

I ask myself what is really wrong, and an answer presents itself. Each of these students is a younger sister of a much-beloved former student. Their big sisters have all graduated after spending three years in my classes. In fact, Jocelyn, Anya's older sister, came to visit just last week, and got an enthusiastic welcome.

"I don't think this is about feeling that I don't like you," I say. "I think this is about your being afraid that I might not end up liking you as much as I like your older sisters. It is true, I am close to Missy, Jocelyn, and Ellie. I had them in my classes for three years. I know them better than I know you, but I have had you for only three weeks. I don't expect you to be just like your sisters, but I expect that I will like you as much as I like them once I get to know you. I think your being mad at me right now is a way to protect yourself from the possibility that I won't like you enough. But you can relax. I like you already, and as we spend more time together, I'll like you even more. Please think about what I have said. I will also think about what you have said."

The girls are surprised. Anya recognizes some truth in it right away, and she stops to give me a hug before she leaves class for lunch. The other two take a little longer to come around, but the four of us ended up having a good three years together.

Today I stopped by school to drop something off. Millie, who is now in high school in Vancouver, is temporarily in San Francisco because her father is dying. I had a good visit with her at school, where she is spending a lot of the time that she is not in the hospital with her father.

*   *   *   *

I am walking along Castro Street, and I run into Janet waiting at the bus stop. She is in her second year of high school and I haven't seen her for awhile. We exchange greetings and hugs. "How is high school?" I ask her. "I don't know," she replies listlessly.

"What's wrong?"

"Well, everybody from our old school seems to be making new friends. Things aren't the same."

"But, Janet," I ask, "aren't you making new friends too?"

"Yeah," she says slowly, "but it's hard."

I know Janet to be a talented, bright, outgoing person. I wait to hear what is wrong. She says, "I don't know, Ms. Logan, it's just that at this school, well, nobody else's mother is gay."

"Oh," I say. "So, how is this for you?"

"It's really hard," Janet tells me. "Most of the kids I know I don't even talk to about it. But I finally made this one new friend in my gym class, so I told her, and, well, she was totally shocked, asking me really naive questions like, 'How did you get born?' and, it's all very depressing. It's not at all like middle school."

"Oh," I say, and we stay quiet for awhile letting the truth of this hang between us. I try some words of comfort. "Well, Janet," I say, "at least you had that safe time, so now when people make naive or thoughtless comments, you know there is something wrong with THEM, not something wrong with YOU."

*   *   *   *

My friend Celeste, who has been in a long-term relationship with another woman, has decided to begin a family. Using the self-insemination program at UC Medical School, she is now pregnant with her first child. While I am visiting her one day, she asks me my opinion on whether or not I feel a child should ever be spanked. I tell her that I do not. We discuss this for awhile, but she seems to still believe that an occassional swat on the behind for emphasis is an okay way to parent.

The next day I tell my sixth graders that my friend, Celeste, is about to become a parent for the first time, and that she is giving a lot of thought to her new role of motherhood. One of the things she is thinking about, I say, is whether or not a child should ever be spanked. She is collecting people's viewpoints in order to help her make a decision. "What did you tell her?" the class asks. "I will tell you my reply," I say, "but first I would like to hear what you think. After all, I am not a parent, and it has been a long time since I have been a child." As we discuss this, a woman walks in and sits down in the back of the room. I am used to having people observe my class, since parents of GATE (Gifted and Talented Education) students can choose the program they wish to send their child to, so between October and January I have many visitors.

The class discusses the issue of whether or not parents should spank their children. Then I ask the students to write Celeste a letter, and to share their ideas and opinions with her. The class settles down into some intense writing; they take this role of adviser seriously, and they set out to convince Celeste that spanking is either okay or not okay.

I ask for volunteers to read their work aloud, and several people share their letters. I listen carefully, learning something about each child's own home discipline system. When the bell rings and the students leave for lunch, I go to the back of the room and introduce myself to the woman who has been observing.

"What a great class," she says. "I wish I had had a teacher like you. My son will be coming to your school next year, and I wanted to see what your class was like. I think he will do fine here. He is not an easy child... he has had some difficulties in school... well, he is not really my son, I am his co-parent." I listen carefully as she decides how much she wants to tell me. Finally she says, "His mother and I are co-parents, we are a two-female family."

"Well," I say, "so is Celeste!" And we both laugh. I reassure her that several of our students come from gay families, and that we are committed to honoring alternative families.

When I give Celeste the stack of letters from the sixth graders, I feel that I am giving her a real gift—the points of view and opinions of children. And I feel that I have given the sixth graders a gift—an attentive audience for their personal ideas and opinions.

*   *   *   *

Frank, my colleague in the GATE program, is delivering some tests to a sixth grade class. On his way out, he notices the doodlings of one of the students. "Why aren't you in my advanced art class?" he asks, and he gets the name and homeroom of the student: Keishon White, 109. Keishon is glad to switch his elective into Frank's class, and Frank continues to recognize and honor his talent. Although Keishon doesn't test high, Frank arranges for him to enter the GATE program. "Keishon needs us," Frank tells me, "and after all, GATE stands for Gifted and Talented, and Keishon is really talented." So Keishon spends the next two years in our program.

One day, as Keishon is drawing a very sexy woman in Frank's art class, Hallie walks by, looks at it, and says, "That's not art, that's sexist trash." Frank puts the picture up on a bulletin board with a sign that says, "Art? or Sexist Trash?" at the top. The class discusses which it is, and why. Everyone who comes into the room over the next few days—parents, student monitors, other teachers, the principal—is drawn into the discussion. Frank keeps a tally under each heading of how many people vote one way or another. It remains a running debate.

When Keishon graduates, he has a large portfolio of work, and he applies to the McAteer School of the Arts. He is accepted.

Some years later, Frank is at the DeYoung Museum, where some of his students are represented in a student art show. "Mr. Foreman, Mr. Foreman," someone calls out from the crowd. It is a very grown up Keishon, who is now a senior. "I have been meaning to visit you," he says. "I just got a full-time art scholarship to the Chicago Art Institute! And I never knew I was an artist until I had your class. Now I have to go out into the world and be an artist, and I have you to blame," he teases.

This is the type of story every teacher cherishes. This one is an example of the importance of the teacher as keen observer—if Frank had not taken the time to glance at Keishon's doodlings, or if he had been too lazy or disconnected to do anything once he had glanced at them, Keishon's life might be very different today. And yet these qualities that make exceptional teachers and exceptional teaching experiences are not on any evaluation form that an administrator can check off, they are not on any standardized test. They just change students' lives.

*   *   *   *

My sixth-graders are listening carefully to a presentation by the people from the Child Abuse Prevention program. The presenters are defining child abuse and teaching the class ways that they can protect themselves. I am sitting in the back of the room, watching. I have a new student who has been in class only a few weeks, and I have been concerned about her. Wandia is the only Hispanic girl in the class, and I haven't noticed the other students making her feel as at home as I would like them to. There is something wild and wonderful about Wandia—she has an intense, angry energy. A slight accent makes her sometimes difficult to understand. One day, after lunch, she hauled off and hit one of the other girls, to get even for the fact that she was excluded from their lunchtime game. Although I physically restrained her, I loved her up-front way of confronting these girls, and the incident gave us a chance to talk about how everyone was feeling. Wandia's self-esteem was clearly intact, and she was not about to take anything from anybody. This, along with her sometimes unruly appearance, frightened some of the other girls, and they excluded her from their lunchtime games by using playground jingles and rhymes, so as to avoid taking any personal responsibility for being cruel. The classroom as global interaction.

As the Child Abuse Prevention presentation continues, Wandia begins to slump in her desk, her head in her hands. I move a little to the side of the room so I can see her face. I see a tear rolling down her cheek. I move to her side and take her by the hand, leading her to the big comfortable couch off to the side of the room. The rest of the class is involved in the presentation, but Wandia sits on the couch next to me and begins to cry. "Would you like to tell me about it?" I ask. She nods. While crying, she says, "It is hard for me to think about what they are talking about, because that is why I am here. We moved here to get away from my uncle, because my mother found out he was sexually abusing my younger sister. We ran away, but he is following us, and we are really scared. The other day when I was leaving school, I saw his truck. We are living over the garage of my grandmother's house until my mother can find a job. My sister cries all the time. She doesn't want to go to school."

She tells me more, then stops and looks at me, part defiant, part relieved, waiting to hear how I will receive this news. "It sounds to me like you could use a big hug," I say, and the defiant part goes away. She nods and she puts her arms around me and cries some more while I hold onto her. When she is finished we go together to see her counselor. We make sure her sister is getting therapy—yes, the whole family is in a program at General Hospital. She brings in a picture of her uncle and shows it to me and to her counselor. "Don't ever let this man take me," she says.

After this, she begins to share parts of her story in class. We are doing a nine-week unit on family life, and as we touch on topics that pertain to Wandia's situation, she talks about abuse. When she does this, it seems as if all the other students freeze, as in a film, and only Wandia and I continue to move and breathe and talk. When she finishes, the students unfreeze and it is as if nothing happened. They are unable to deal with her story. I try to model for them a caring, accepting and supportive audience for Wandia's story.

I make a point of spending time with her each day. One Monday she comes to school very upset. Her uncle had kidnapped her mother over the weekend, and tried to strangle her, but her mother had escaped. "We have a restraining order," she tells me. "Are you feeling frightened?" I ask. "Not while I am in school," she says. "I keep my mind off it. But I am frightened when I am at home." She tells me that her sister sits on the floor of the bathroom with her head on the toilet seat cover, and cries all the time. "We got her one of those fuzzy covers for the toilet, to make her feel better," she says.

She and her mother plan a surprise birthday party for her sister. Wandia is excited and enthused. When she returns after the weekend of the party, I ask her how it went. "Fine, until my sister's friend got shot." "What do you mean?" I ask. I remember reading in the newspaper that a young girl was killed in a random shooting while walking along the street. "She shouldn't have walked by those projects," Wandia says.

*   *   *   *

I am teaching the same Family Life unit to the seventh and eighth graders in the afternoon. This is a class for everyone who didn't get Family Life in the sixth grade—either they were in another teacher's class who didn't do it, or they transferred in from another school. I distribute a Dear Abby-type letter in class. This letter is written by a seventeen year old girl. In it she says that she and her boyfriend are thinking of having sexual intercourse. They both will be going to college in the fall, and it is unthinkable to them that she might get pregnant. Nevertheless, they seem to be getting closer and closer to having sexual intercourse.

The assignment is for the students to read the letter and then to write a careful answer. After some writing time, I ask students to share their answers with the class. Most answers involve detailed instructions about various birth control methods, the significance of nonoxynol-nine, where to purchase birth control devices, how to use them, and admonishments about never having sex without using a condom. Melissa raises her hand. "But the girl writing this letter said she was just THINKING about having sex," Melissa says, "She didn't say she was GOING to have sex. Why is everyone talking about birth control when all she said was that she was thinking about it? When I am flying in an airplane, I THINK about what it would be like to open the cabin door and watch all the papers, seats and people be sucked out of the plane, but I would never DO it."

For Melissa, having sex is as preposterous and as dangerous as opening a plane door at 32,000 feet. On the other hand, Kerry asks to speak to me after class. We go to sit on the couch, so we can be comfortable and so I can give her my full attention. This classroom couch is a time-out place, and the unwritten law there is that when we sit on the couch, we become two human beings, instead of a teacher and a student. We also become invisible to the rest of the class, so that it is okay to cry, complain, laugh, or lie down for a nap—the class continues on. But in this case, it is after school, and Kerry and I are alone.

"I don't like this class," she tells me. "I want to switch classes."

"Okay. Tell me why."

"This class is going to be about whether or not to use drugs, whether or not to have sex. I already have a lot of experience with drugs, and I have a lot of experience with sex, so I think this class will be boring for me."

"Hmm. I see your point, but I disagree with you. You weren't here on the first day of school when I talked about the plans for this class, but you should know that I feel that my responsibility as your teacher is to bring in all the latest information on sexually transmitted diseases, on birth control methods, on AIDS, and on other subjects. We will have about twenty guest lecturers in this class, and each lecturer will be an expert in his or her field. It seems to me that this is the perfect class for you. As a sexually active person you deserve all the latest information you can get. Also, Kerry, this class is about making choices and decisions. If you have strong feelings and a lot of experiences, it seems to me that you can be a great resource for the rest of the class. Besides, choices and decisions are never final—we continue making them all of our lives. You might even find that this class influences you to change your mind about some things."

She thinks about what I have said. "It's not really that," she says. "What it really is is that I am jealous of the other kids. They have parents who care about what they do and who watch out for them. I've never had anybody really watch out for me. Now that I am in therapy, I understand that I should have had a lot of parenting that I never got. It will be painful for me to be in this class."

"You have done a lot of work in therapy in a very short time," I tell her. "I'm really moved that you are able to articulate how you are really feeling. I am proud of you. You will be an asset to this class. I wouldn't want to do it without you."

Kerry stays in Family Life. We have two evening sessions for students and their parents. Kerry attends both sessions, and I act as her parent.

*   *   *   *

There are thirty-two students in this class. Each student has a story (as I write this I hear the music from *Dragnet* in the background—dum da dum dum). I told one about Melissa, and one about Kerry, to illustrate how different they are. One curriculum does not fit all. Also, when teachers complain about class size going up, I believe they are really lamenting their growing inability to learn each child's story, and to tailor the curriculum in such a way as to fit the needs of each one. The more children in a class, the more necessary it is to have just one story. But how can one curriculum respond to both a Melissa and a Kerry? The answer to that, I think, is that they both get left out.

*   *   *   *

It is the day after Halloween. We are to practice descriptive writing. I walk the students out of the building and down a short alley to nearby Mission Dolores. We go through the Mission and out into the graveyard. The assignment is that the students have twenty minutes to silently observe the details of the graveyard, and to take notes. When we return to class, we will write a show-not-tell paper describing the Mission cemetery. I sit on a marble slab in the sunlight, watching the students quietly scurrying around, copying down the names and inscriptions and dates on grave-stones, listing the plants and animals they see and hear, listing the colors, the smells, the textures. Twenty minutes turns into forty minutes, but they are so absorbed I hate to cut them short. When we finally return to class, they share details eagerly, they write great descriptions.

Next, I decide to let them do comparison papers, building on their descriptive techniques. Frank has a second period prep time, so I bring them to his classroom during second period. He has the most interesting room I have ever seen. It is full of distractions. "You have twenty minutes to silently take notes on Mr. Foreman's room," I tell them. "The assignment will be to write a paper telling what his room says about him as a person." Some students begin to wander around, writing down slogans, copying down poems, listing book titles. Others sit in their seats, craning their necks to count the forty-seven clocks, broken televisions, the chairs hanging on the wall.

Later in class, they write magnificent papers. We give them to Frank for Christmas. Then I say, "Now look at my room, and write a paper telling how my room says different things about me than Mr. Foreman's does about him." We have fun with these papers.

Another descriptive writing assignment that is fun:

"Change your seat so you are sitting across from someone you don't know very well," I tell them. "Now, describe everything you can about how that person looks. Be specific." After the class finishes, I collect the papers and redistribute them at random. The task is to find the person being described in the paper. Or, sometimes we draw a picture according to the description, then try to match the picture to the person.

*   *   *   *

Frank tells me the Geoffrey Wong story: One day, when Frank was teaching in another middle school, he came to realize that he had had a student in his Art class for three years, and he didn't really know him. This student was never absent from school. He completed every assignment, and each assignment was always turned in on time. He was quiet and well-behaved in class. But he never got any attention, either positive or negative. So Frank planned a Geoffrey Wong Day, to celebrate this student before he left the school. His students made a big banner that said "Geoffrey Wong Day." They baked a cake with his name on it. He was the center of attention in class. Frank brought him around the school, introducing Geoffrey to his counselor, the dean, and the principal, all of whom did not know him. Geoffrey Wong was King for a Day. I love this story of a teacher turning an invisible student into a visible one. I believe this endeared Frank to all the Geoffery Wongs in his classes.

*   *   *   *

Kathie, who shares my classroom with me, has a particularly needy student named Emilio. One day he says to her, "Teacher, today it is my birthday." Kathie gives him a big hug, she wishes him a happy birthday, and she gives him special privileges for the day. Emilio sits smiling and pleased. Three or four weeks later, Emilio says shyly, "Teacher, today it is my birthday." Kathie again gives him special birthday attention. Every four or five weeks during the remainder of the year, Emilio announces his birthday. Kathie, who teaches math, never points out to him that it is impossible to age seven or eight years during seventh grade. She just keeps on giving those hugs.

american women making history

WHEN MY NIECE, Hannah, was twelve years old—
that age when young girls feel the need to separate from mothers and other
significant female role models—she announced to me with a trace of defi-
ance, "Auntie Judy, I know that you are a feminist, and I feel that I should
tell you that I am not one."

Now, Hannah and I have always been close, and I have always been one
of her confidants. She telephones me to read me her writing before she turns
in her homework, and I am one of her biggest fans. She calls me to complain
when her older brother doesn't do his share of cleaning the bathroom.
When she argues with her step-mother, I listen to her side of the story.

"Really, Hannah?" I say. "What has brought you to the decision that you
are not a feminist?"

Hannah pauses. I think she expected me to argue with her, or to be
disappointed in her. But I am simply asking her to tell me more about her
thoughts. "Well," she says, "I guess I'm not one because I don't really know
what it means."

"That sounds very wise of you," I say, "not to describe yourself as something when you are not sure what it means. Actually, many people define
'feminist' in many different ways. The definition I use, when I talk about
it in the classroom, is that a feminist is a man or a woman who believes
that both males and females should have equal rights and responsibilities
in both the public and private domains, and who is willing to act on those
beliefs. In other words, not only should you be able to run for President of
the United States just as easily as your brother, Josh, but he should have
equal responsibility for cleaning up the bathroom you two share."

Hannah pauses a moment to let this sink in.

"I am one," she declares. And she has been one, ever since.

I tell this story because I think a lot of students, and other people too,
come to the classroom with misinformation about what it means to have
a feminist classroom, or to include women in the curriculum. Like Hannah,
they dissociate themselves from what they don't understand.

When I present workshops on feminist curriculum, I am always asked questions like, "But what do the BOYS do while you are sewing quilts?" And some people seem surprised that the boys are sewing, too.

Or they ask, "But how do the boys in the classroom feel when you are studying women?"

To me, these questions indicate many misconceptions. First of all, women have benefited in schools for many, many years by studying the lives, values, and experiences of men. I think men can benefit just as much from studying about the lives, values, and experiences of women. Second, women's lives need to be presented without apology. They need to be presented as one half of the world's experience. It is only when they are presented as "lesser," that the boys don't want to do it. And when they are presented as "lesser," girls don't want to do it either. And I don't blame them.

But my workshop audience persists. "Don't the boys EVER object?" they want to know. So to make them feel better, I tell them the story of Pablo, who did object.

Pablo was a sixth grader when we were studying a unit on Women in Comparative Societies, which focused on women in Saudi Arabia, Israel, the United States, and Sweden. We began by looking at how women achieved status in these cultures, and from there we proceeded to look at many aspects of each culture, from family law to religious values. By focusing on how women gained status in these four cultures we learned about family life, public policy regarding women and children, and domestic values, as well as the traditional information about the public world of government, finances, and so forth.

Pablo was the third son in a single parent family, and I had had his older brother Chris in my class some years before. One evening his mother telephoned, shortly after I had sent home an interim warning informing her that Pablo was missing several homework assignments. I was glad to hear from her, and frankly, I thought she was calling to thank me, as the day before Pablo and three other boys had come to my home for a tea party. We baked cookies and had a nice visit, and I drove them each home, since it was raining rather hard.

But I was unprepared for her anger. She asked me if I was teaching what I "was supposed to," since Pablo complained to her that we were studying about women, and she was concerned that he wouldn't learn the "real curriculum." I replied that Pablo was indeed learning the "real curriculum," and that if she sat down and talked to him about what we were doing, I thought she would find solid lessons there in history, comparative religion, etc. But, I explained, we are entering these lessons through the female experience, so actually Pablo is having something added to his education, not something subtracted. I explained that as a student of a Mentor Teacher, Pablo was part of a pilot program in my class. (My Mentor Teacher project was to develop and collect materials on including women in curriculum.) "Actually, Pablo is very lucky," I say. "He's getting something extra. Most curriculum today still includes only the male perspective."

But I agree that we should have a conference "with the counselor and the principal," as requested. I think the Real Problem here, I say, is that Pablo somehow thinks that when we study women, it is not really school work.

We arrange a time and place for the conference. Pablo's mother leaves me with the distinct feeling that I am "in trouble." I hang up the phone and unplug it, wanting no more parent conferences that night, thank you. I cry and feel sorry for myself. Here I am, baking cookies, driving kids home in the rain, knocking myself out not to be just a textbook teacher, and this is what I get. I soak in a hot tub and plan "my side" of the impending conference, since it already feels like an unfriendly win/lose ordeal.

About ten-thirty, I plug the phone back in and it immediately starts ringing. I am surprised when I answer that it is Pablo's mother.

"I am so glad you answered the phone," she says. "I have called to apologize. I did as you suggested, I sat down and talked to Pablo about what he has been doing in your class. You are right, he is learning many things that are important. And he is also learning about women's lives and experiences. Here I am, a working mother trying to raise three sons, and you are teaching about me, about my life. I am so sorry I gave you a bad time. I hope you will forgive me."

I am friendly on the phone and "forgive her," and inside I think to myself, don't forget this moment. A bit ago you felt AWFUL. Now you feel TERRIFIC. Pablo's mother was unsupportive only because she didn't understand. She wants to cancel our appointment, but I encourage her to keep it so we can help Pablo get his work in.

At the time, Pablo was a difficult child, and needed BOTH his mother and his teacher to help him mature. I had Pablo for three years, and he did grow up, in many ways. But I never forgot that early experience, which started out feeling so unpleasant and ended up feeling so good. A few days before his graduation from middle school, I asked Pablo if I could interview him about his experiences at school. He seemed delighted. I asked him many questions, one of which was, "Now that you are going to high school, you may or may not have teachers that include women in curriculum. If they do not, do you think you would ever choose to do reading or research on women if it were not an explicit part of the assignment?"

"Oh, sure," Pablo responds easily. "Especially on Demeter. Demeter's stories are my favorite."

Pablo's story has echoed Hannah's.

I think that some people are afraid that, because (men's) history excluded women for so long, somehow women's history is about excluding men, or replacing men, which it is not. I am aware, however, that by focusing on women for two or three assignments a year (the NOW essay contest and the quilt), and by including women in many other assignments (Black History month), I am seen as being very extreme, whereas many teachers focus only on men's experience for the entire year, and this is seen as "normal."

If my class seems anxious at the beginning of a "woman's unit," I reassure them that women's studies is not about "ruling over," it is about "existing with." It is important to be explicit with these reassurances right away. Feminist teaching is not about allowing a win/lose situation to develop between boys and girls.

I teach my sixth grade class for three periods in the morning—Language Arts, Reading, and Social Studies. In the afternoon, I teach seventh and eighth graders, half of whom are my former sixth graders, for a two period block of English/Social Studies core courses. Sometimes I teach a unit for a whole semester, sometimes I teach nine-week units, sometimes I teach two one-hour electives. Since I team plan with three other teachers, we have a lot of flexibility in our scheduling. We like combining the seventh and eighth graders as it gives us more choices in meeting their needs.

One year we focus on Global Studies, the next year we focus on American Studies. So each student gets everything, eventually. But as seventh and eighth graders, they can, with parental guidance, chose which teacher and which unit suits them best. During the American Studies year, I teach a five-week, two hour a day class called "American Women Making History."

I have a lot of concerns about this class. How can I, in five weeks, do justice to the regional, ethnic, racial, economic and cultural diversity of women in American history? How can I include women from all aspects of life—private and public—so that students expand their notions of what history is? How can I cover not only the last two hundred years, but the hundreds of years before that that women lived and worked on this soil? How can I make this class fun and exciting so that students will internalize a love of history and research that will not self-destruct in five weeks?

Fortunately, because I have been a Mentor Teacher for the last several years and have had a supplementary budget for materials, I have many books by and about women in my classroom. In fact, when students enter my room for the first time, they often look around at all the shelves and displays of books, and ask meekly, "Are we going to have to read all this?"

I quickly explain that my classroom is a resource center for other teachers and students, and that while they are free to read and use the books in the room, they certainly will not be expected to read them all.

I have collected many examples of curriculum from other districts. I am not lacking for materials. Assuredly I could keep them mighty busy reading, writing, and memorizing for the next five weeks. But I don't want my students to be consumers of curriculum. I want them to be producers of curriculum.

In each class, I have students with a diversity of interests, abilities, talents, learning styles, and something that I think in kindergarten they call "emotional readiness." What works for one student doesn't necessarily work for another. When I think of curriculum, I picture a journey. In traditional curriculum, everyone is supposed to be on the same journey at the same time, and the teacher's role is like that of a sheep dog, trying to keep everyone together. It is like being on a field trip, always looking ahead to one group of students and saying, "Wait for us, don't get on that streetcar, we're not all there yet," and then looking behind, saying, "Hurry up, walk faster, we'll never get there at this pace." And I think of feminist curriculum as a journey that acknowledges that, while everyone needs to be moving forward, most of us are in different places at different times. Some people are filling out passport applications; some people are touring beautiful cathedrals and famous monuments; some people are sitting in cafes having bread and cheese and intense conversations; some people are learning Japanese; some are homesick, writing letters home; some are putting together their photo albums. The teacher's role in this vision becomes one of keen observer. After all, it is inappropriate to speak Japanese to someone who is filling out a passport application, and it is inappropriate to hand a photo album to someone eating and visiting in a cafe. This metaphor seems to capture my impression of the difference between traditional teach-and-test curriculum and student-centered curriculum that acknowledges the individual interests, talents, and learning styles in the class.

Thinking about one of my curriculum guidelines—that is, if I control the content, you get to control the form; if I control the form, you get to control the content—I decide to make the content (women in history) the "have to" part of the class, and the form the "get to" part of the class.

So I talk to the students about how they will be doing a project in this class. They may work alone or in a group (not more than four to a group). They may choose one aspect of women in history to research in depth, such as women in sports or drama, or dance, or social reform. Or, they may choose to research one group of women's experience, such as Chinese immigrants to California, or the Filipina American experience. Or, they may focus on one time frame or regional frame, like Women in the West.

They must present their findings to the class, first researching their topic in depth, then creating a presentation that allows us to share what they have learned. We will each be both teacher and learner. We won't pretend to cover it all. The class presentation may include a dramatic skit, it may be in the form of a comic book, a mural, a Judy Chicago *Dinner Party* (using paper plates instead of porcelain), a board game, a children's book, complete with illustrations, and so forth. We spend some time discussing our options. I show slides of former student presentations for inspiration.

Some students know immediately what they want to do. Others need more guidance. When students come up with ideas for their own projects, I try to say yes frequently.

Now, students at this age (or at any age, really) may look askance at women in history (the "have to" part), but they are suckers for making comic books, playing music, painting murals, or acting out (the "get to" part). When they hear that they can include art, drama, and music, they are hooked.

Suddenly this sounds like fun. We go to the local libraries, the school libraries, and discover that they don't have as many books on women as our classroom does (thank you, Mentor Teacher Program and San Francisco Education Foundation, for the grants enabling me to purchase so many materials by and about women). The students are shocked. They begin to understand that something is being left out.

I help them narrow down their topics into reasonable chunks, and they begin scanning indexes and tables of contents for information. We also talk about primary research, and they begin to set up interviews. (A teacher friend, whose daughter is in my class, teases me for years later about the phone bill she received when her daughter Lena called her uncle in North Carolina so her best friend could interview him about his horse farm.)

Students work in small groups around the room. Some sit on the floor reading quietly. Others go behind the filing cabinets to rehearse skits. Others are making puppets, painting murals, cutting things out. I devote about a third of the class time to this research/project activity.

During the other two-thirds I read to them. I show videos and movies, mostly ordered from Project SEE (Seeking Educational Equity) in Sacramento, a branch of the California state government committed to providing audio-visual materials about women to classrooms. (One phones and orders materials for a specific date, and they are mailed free of charge. One pays only for return postage.) This way I am able to show movies like *One Fine Day, Rosie the Riveter, Women of Summer,* and *Still Killing Us Softly.* Students begin to expand their notions of women in history beyond Betsy Ross.

We read "A Five Minute Summary of Seventy Five Years," and talk about what is "real work." I talk to them about Peggy McIntosh's theories of including women in curriculum. An over-simplification of her Phase Theory hangs on the wall of our classroom. We begin to use her terminology in class. I show segments of *Eyes on the Prize* and *Slaying the Dragon.* We read poems, letters, and short stories written by women of color. I show video segments of *Famous Americans* on Elizabeth Cady Stanton, Susan B. Anthony, Sojourner Truth, Harriet Tubman, Eleanor Roosevelt, Elizabeth Blackwell, Margaret Sanger, Helen Keller, Georgia O'Keeffe, and others. We listen to songs about Sybil Ludington, Harriet Tubman, and Gertrude Ederle. We listen to the music of Sweet Honey in the Rock, and we discuss the lyrics. We ask ourselves, who are we leaving out?

In the fourth week, we begin our class presentations. It is time to teach each other, and I am unprepared for how wonderful the students' projects are. Most presentations are much longer than I expected. Students have come up with creative ideas beyond my imagination. I am thrilled. In the end, I have to ask the other three teachers for an extra two days before we switch classes.

Some students do a traditional oral presentation of a research report on one outstanding woman—Eleanor Roosevelt, or Sojourner Truth. That indicates where these students are on their journeys: school means carefully fulfilling someone else's expectations. But most students have somehow put their own creative signature on their projects.

Hallie has created several small cardboard statues of liberty, holding up the freedom flame. On the face of each, she has pasted the picture of one of the women she is reporting on. She holds up each statue as she tells the story of that woman's life: Sarah Winnemucca, holding a book that says "Indian Rights"; Barbara Jordan, holding a book that says "Civil Rights"; Mother Jones, holding a book that says "Workers' Rights"; Sojourner Truth, holding a book that says "Women's Rights"; and finally, with flame-colored hair, Cyndi Lauper, holding a book that says "Individual Rights."

Anat and Diane have taken a cardboard box and constructed a television set. They have used a long piece of paper, wound around two dowels, to turn the images on the "screen." Their topic is women in literature, and they talk about Tillie Olsen, Virginia Woolf, Kate Chopin, Alice Walker and Willa Cather.

Another student has also constructed a TV set out of a box. He reports on Amelia Earhart as he turns the paper on the "screen." We see Amelia's baby footprint, her first plane with a price tag on it, a map of the United States tracing her first transcontinental journey.

Four of my male students have put many hours into constructing a Jeopardy game on Women in History. Students are delighted and respond favorably to $50, $500, and $5,000 questions. The boys have spent their own money on candy prizes.

Four female students have set up a Judy Chicago *Dinner Party*, drawing the faces of several women on paper plates, placing cards next to the settings, and talking about these women's lives as the class walks around their table.

Dan and Abraham, our class artists, work together on a comic book called, "Two Women Written Back Into History," about Harriet Tubman and Sojourner Truth. They are proud of their work and share it eagerly with the class. I photograph them.

Annette and Zoe come up with another original project. Struck by the quote from the UN Decade for Women that frames one of my classroom walls ("Women are one-half of the world's population, they do two-thirds of the world's work, they earn one-tenth of the world's income, they own one-hundredth of the world's property"), they borrow Annette's uncle's video camera. Each Saturday, they go to one or two different neighborhoods in the city, planning carefully to visit a diversity of neighborhoods. They take turns "manning" the camera. They are both novices, so the resulting footage is sometimes a bit wobbly. The interviewer politely asks strangers on the street if he or she will help them with a homework assignment. When the subject agrees, they state the UN statistics and ask for a response. Most people have never heard the statistics before, and they respond with interest, telling personal stories about why they think it is true. Most are delighted with the assignment. "I never got to do anything like this when I was in school," is a frequent comment.

Watching this video takes a long time. Annette and Zoe have not learned about editing. But their enthusiasm for this project infects the class, and we spend several class days watching and talking about the footage. "Wait until you see what happened at the financial district," they tell us. And sure enough, at one of the convention centers, a bus pulls up, and Zoe asks the tourists to respond to the quote. One man is pretty intoxicated, and he uses this opportunity to impress his friends by saying some ugly and oppressive things about women. He goes on and on. He does not swear, but he says terrible things.

The girls bravely keep on filming.

"How did you feel when this was happening?" I ask the girls.

"We couldn't BELIEVE that he was saying such things, but we were so excited to be getting footage of it!! We knew just telling you about it wouldn't work—we wanted the class to be able to SEE it." Like professionals, they didn't let their personal feelings interfere with taping the interview.

Zeb, a student I have been worried about for sometime, makes a board game on Harriet Tubman. He has a great time doing it. But the game cards say things like "The sheriff found you in the swamp, go to jail." Or, "Whoops, you took a wrong turn, forfeit your chance to go north." The art work is nice, I say to Zeb, but it doesn't reflect Harriet Tubman's real life. She was never caught—she never lost a passenger. She never had to go to jail. Zeb did the "get to" without doing the "have to" (in this case, proper research).

Other students construct board games. One is on Women in the Olympics, and players are given little cardboard female signs (circles with a plus) for markers.

Amelia decides to do a report on the Triangle Shirtwaist Fire. She does extensive research and ties the incident into the larger theme of worker rights and social reform. At the same time, she constructs a large model of the Triangle Building. From the top three floors, with yellow and red paper she depicts fire coming out of the windows. Her report is dramatic and effective.

Some time later, I run into Amelia's mother, who is also a teacher, at the local supermarket. She tells me that her husband is an architect, and that while her son had often worked with his Dad in his office, this project was the first time that Amelia had done so. Amelia learned to use his tools and talked to him about his skills as she made her miniature building.

Students begin to get a sense of the richness of women's studies. They say things like, "Why didn't I ever hear of her before?" Or, "How come this isn't in the books?" They get all kinds of ideas from each other. Sometimes my giving verbal permission isn't enough—they need to see other students doing art projects or video tapes before they get a sense of what it can look like. Sometimes, those students who write traditional essays on one woman ask to do their project over once they see what other students have done.

The year we center on American Studies, I offer other elective classes: American Poetry, American Biographies, American Short Stories. Before each class, I consider how to include Phase Four curriculum. In the poetry class, I include many poems by women.

Rosie is intrigued with the poem, "Two Gretels," by Robin Morgan. She decides she would like to paint a watercolor of this poem. Since she is in my homeroom every morning, I invite her to bring her watercolors to class and to paint during the fifteen minutes every morning that we spend on sustained silent reading (this is a school policy—everyone from janitors to students is supposed to read quietly during this time; like Sleeping Beauty's castle falling asleep for a hundred years, we read) to paint instead. None of the other students complain as Rosie works diligently each day on her painting. They continue to read quietly. Rosie produces a lovely work of art. Her art teacher and I frame it for her, and give it to her for a graduation present.

I want to say a word here about saying "Yes" to the passions of individual students. I can hear someone being critical, saying, "But all the children are SUPPOSED to be reading, why should ONE be allowed to paint? Shouldn't they ALL be allowed to paint if Rosie gets to?" (Perhaps this critical voice that I hear is an aspect of myself and maybe that's why I need to pause a moment to answer it.) In response, I say that students seem to understand that by saying yes to one student's needs, I am in a way saying yes to all their possibilities too. Unlike some adults, they seem to understand that everyone has different interests, needs, talents, abilities, and gifts. I would be remiss if I let the whole class paint during Sustained Silent Reading. After all, the Curriculum Committee has voted that this is what we are supposed to be doing during this time. But I don't feel remiss in letting Rosie paint. She is a straight "A" student who already reads tons. But with her demanding schedule, this painting will not come to life without this gift of time. The students in her class understand this.

Rosie's painting is an example of what can happen when teachers give students permission to follow their own visions. This philosophy also enables students to include their own stories in their work. Students need to feel connected to what they are doing, either by being allowed to discuss their own experiences and feelings, or by being allowed to express what they have learned in a way that is meaningful to them, as in art or drama.

In the American Biographies class, we begin with biographies of people in our own families. Students interview and write about their grandparents, parents, or aunts and uncles, and do an oral report in class as well as a written report. We learn about grandmothers and assorted family members.

Ellie tells of her Irish grandmother in Brooklyn, who, distressed that her oldest son had married a non-Catholic girl, one day spontaneously baptised her two granddaughters in the kitchen sink.

Anat tells us about her Jewish grandmother in Brooklyn. She was making chicken soup one day, and her several children were playing on the kitchen floor. The laundry was hung out to dry off the fire escape, and someone on the roof of the tenement threw away a lighted cigar, which landed on the laundry and set it on fire. Anat's grandmother thought quickly and doused the fire with the chicken soup.

Hua writes about his father and tells us about the significance of his father's name. While the last name is a common family name in Vietnam, his father's first name means "high value" or "law." Hua writes that this name carries a permanent message from his grandparents to his father.

He goes on to describe his father's education and career as an English teacher, the Vietnam war, and his family's escape by boat in the middle of the night. They were rescued by an Indonesian ship after five days on the open seas, just as their food and water were running out. After some time in a refugee camp, they came to San Francisco, where they first stayed in an uncle's basement in Daly City. Eventually, they found a place of their own, and Hua's father now teaches English in a high school in San Francisco.

Students learn a lot from this American Biography, and Hua's story becomes a window for us to look through, experiencing his life with him. Later, Hua is elected student body president of our school. The diversity of our class comes into focus.

The stories are too numerous for me to report here. But the assignment gives students opportunities to interview and celebrate members of their own families, and as we learn more about each other, we like each other better.

We also often learn more about ourselves. Ellie comes back to visit after graduation. I am applying for a grant, and I ask her to write me a letter of recommendation. In this letter, among other things, she says that while she knew her Canadian grandmother well, this assignment had given her the opportunity to find out about her American grandmother, and to claim a part of her heritage that had been in the shadows.

I particularly enjoy teaching American Short Stories, and find that this class gives me lots of opportunities for Phase Four curriculum. For example, we read Maureen Daly's award-winning story, "Sixteen," and discuss it in class. The students love it. I ask them to write a story with their own age as the title, and to capture the spirit of their own age in the same way that Maureen Daly has captured the spirit of being a sixteen-year-old girl.

Hallie, Rosie's younger sister, writes the following story:

TWELVE

Buddy Holly crooned in the darkened room. Ninth and eleventh graders flirted and fought. A couple slammed a door behind them. It was an end-of-school party, and I had somehow been cool enough to get invited.

The bright birds at the party were two sophisticated McAteer boys, in black suits (it was formal), slicked back (or up, as the case may be) hair and long, thin cigarettes. After standing around for a time, self-consciously talking and preening with the older kids, one of the "smoothies" asked me to dance.

Surprised, I went out and we danced, long and close. It was quite a different experience from dancing with bashful junior high boys. Afterwards, I sat down, legs crossed just right, and we talked softly for awhile. Then (Heaven!), we danced again. He stood with his arm around me. I was confused. Was he just fooling around? Did he like me? I responded eagerly, and after a time we were "an item" at the party.

I'm afraid I looked at him adoringly the whole time. As we stood in the darkened hallway outside of the dancing room, he asked me my name. I had forgotten to tell him. His arm was comfortable and familiar, the lights soft and shiny, Buddy Holly's voice sweeter than ever.

"Anna," I said softly.

"Hey, you're Amy's sister!" I nodded. "I thought she said her sister was twelve!"

I sighed, and came out of the softness of this fantasy. His arm was gone, the lights seemed to reflect in their glare all my youth and inadequacy, and Buddy Holly sounded resentful as if he, too, had been deceived.

"That's me," I said quietly. He didn't act shocked or angry, he just casually moved away. I realized that with all his sophistication and experience, it meant nothing to him. While I, with all my pent-up adolescence that had been waiting so long, set free and shot down, I was crushed. And so comes the great change. I no longer have rosy images of romance under friendly stars, and the pain is dulled, but I will never feel the same.

Not everyone writes such a descriptive piece. But everyone thinks about and writes about the quintessence of being eleven or twelve.

We read Alice Walker's "Everyday Use," and Dorothy Canfield's "The Bedquilt." Each story offers us an opportunity to write about aspects of ourselves, so the students do this by writing about artifacts of family history in their homes.

On alternate years we study Global History. During these years I have taught many classes in Greek mythology, as well as units on India; Southeast Asia; Shakespeare; Fairy Tales; Rites of Passage; *Moon, Moon*; and

Victorian novels. Each class combines reading, writing, research and social studies. As I teach each class, I try to incorporate inclusive curriculum and Phase Four theory into the lesson.

In the *Moon, Moon* class, I use Anne Kent Rush's book of the same title as the text. This book is a collection of facts, poems, stories, fables, myths, articles and essays about the moon. Ms. Rush's contention is that any given society's attitudes towards the moon also reflect their attitudes about women. She collected all the information about the moon from as many cultures around the world as she could. We discuss this theory in class, and decide to explore her ideas and test them for ourselves. One of our homework assignments is to look at the moon every night. We talk about everything from lunacy to the dimensions of moon craters. We also agree to do a special project about the moon. Meanwhile, class time is spent reading poetry, stories, myths, and science, and writing our own stories, poems and myths about the moon. One day, a parent drops by to visit. She happens to be an expert astrologer and tarot card reader. She stays to talk about the moon in astrology.

Natis constructs a wonderful mobile. Enameled discs depict the phases of the moon in order: waxing, full, waning, and dark. Cybelle sews a Moon Goddess costume. It is a long dark blue gown with seed pearls sewn onto it. Her close-fitting blue cap has a silver satin stuffed new moon perched on it, standing up straight, like a crown. I am surprised, because Cybelle is so shy, but she wears this costume to class with great dignity. Lynette collects songs about the moon and makes a special tape of this collection: "Moon Over Miami," "Blue Moon," "Shine On Harvest Moon," "How High the Moon," etc. Some of the best student short stories I've ever read come out of this class. This class reminds me that curriculum does not have to be either/or, as in either science or art, either facts or fantasy, but can be both/and, as in both about space and about ourselves, both about learning and about having fun.

angela's ritual

ONE YEAR WHEN planning electives with a global emphasis in English and Social Studies, I decided to teach a class called Rites of Passage. My intention was to develop a class that honored the middle school child's need to understand the role of ritual in daily life, and to introduce each student to a cross-cultural awareness of how humans celebrate universal events such as birth, coming of age, marriage, healing, holidays, and death.

Since I believe that modeling is effective teaching, and since this class was to be about researching and experiencing ritual, I began with an initiation ritual that initiated the students into the class. I asked them to bring an object that they cherished to class. We moved the chairs and tables aside, sat in a circle on the carpeted floor, and began by going around the circle, giving each student an opportunity to put her/his cherished object in the middle of the circle, telling us what it was and why it was special. I explained, as best I could, the Native American belief in the power of the four directions, and we honored the power of the East, South, West, and North. We also lit a candle to represent fire, incense to represent air, and we had a bowl of water and a rock and flowers to represent earth.

I asked the students to go around the circle and talk about different groups they belonged to, or different roles that were a part of their identitites. "For example," I began, "I am a teacher, a friend, a daughter, a sister, a union member, an aunt." Each student defined herself/himself ("I am a Boy Scout, forward on the basketball team, a member of the Filipino Club"). "This ritual was to initiate you into this class," I told them. "Look around the room," I said, "we will be together like a kind of family for nine weeks. We will never be together in quite this same way again. We each have our unique, individual selves, and we are each now part of this group." To ritually represent these ideas, I brought a large skein of red yarn. We went around the circle, and each student wrapped this yarn around the left wrist of the person sitting on her left, and said, "This is to represent that you are woven into this group." When we were all looped together, I then passed around a pair of scissors, and as each student cut the yarn for the person on her left, she said, "This is to represent that you are also unique, you are your own person." When we finished, I suggested that they tie a knot in their red yarn bracelet, and wear it throughout our time together as a tangible symbol of our class. They did so.

I was surprised at the power of this ritual. I don't think I've ever seen a class focus and bond so quickly. The next assignment called for the students to form groups of six, and decide what rite of passage they would be responsible for researching. Their task was to look at many cultures, and to report their findings back to class. The second part of this assignment was to provide some kind of ritual for the class that embodied the group's research. This ritual could involve food, music, guided fantasy, etc.

*　　　　*　　　　*　　　　*

It has been eight years since I taught this class, but I have vivid memories of the commitment of the students, the rituals they provided, the wealth of information they collected. Each group presented a formal research report as well as a ritual. One group researched daily life rituals—how different cultures treated the cooking and serving of food, getting up and going to bed, saying hello and saying good-bye, greeting guests, and so on. One group researched seasonal holidays, and we also had groups on birth, death, marriage, coming of age, and mental or physical crises.

Lea was one of my best students. She had lost one of the members of her household to AIDS, and she had other family friends who were dying of AIDS. She was the chair of the death group. Not only did she do significant research on a variety of attitudes and customs about death in the USSR, Mexico, China, some African tribes, Japan and Ireland, but she led us in a very powerful ritual where she took us on a guided fantasy and asked us to imagine our own deaths. I admit this made me nervous. I was afraid some of my students might become frightened or upset. So when the guided fantasy was over, I asked that we go around the circle and check in, telling something about how we were feeling, or how the experience was for us. I was amazed at how calm and clear everybody was, and how their "death experience" reflected something about who they already were. Meg, for example, was still a very playful pre-adolescent. "I imagined myself on a fluffy, comfortable cloud," she reported, "happily bouncing up and down, and looking down on earth at all my friends and family, knowing I could play tricks on them." Nobody was upset or scared. This class taught me to trust this process more than I already had.

Rosie designed a coming of age greeting card. She painted a picket fence with a pink rose bush growing on one side, about to turn a corner. This watercolor painting had a poem inside:

> How quickly the years have passed
> Since I first planted my little rose bush.
> She was frail and delicate and

We weren't always sure
She'd make it through winter.
But look at her,
She's covered
A good third of the fence
Her roots have thickened
And she's started to bloom.

Students wore their red-yarn bracelets throughout the class. One of the students was taken out of school near the end of the class, as her mother had decided to move to a small town in Northern California. This student was reluctant to make this move, and was feeling very sad about leaving. She had some good friends in our program, so over the next year I used to ask about her and send greetings through her friends. A year later she came to visit one of these friends for a week, and she came to spend a few days at our school. When she came to my room I gave her a big hug, and with a great smile, she pulled back her sleeve to show me that her red-yarn bracelet was still tied around her left wrist.

It was shortly after this class that Angela approached me one day and said we needed to talk. "I haven't started my period yet," Angela said, "but when I do, I would like you to do a menstruation ritual for me. I have spoken to my parents about this, and they think it's a great idea."

I am delighted and honored, and I tell her so. I ask her what she has in mind. "I will leave the ritual up to you," she says. "I don't want to have it until I have actually started menstruating. I want both my parents there, and some of my best friends, and I would like to invite Mr. Foreman."

Angela is a seventh grader when she makes this request. For the next few months her upcoming ritual is something to anticipate. When she returns from Winter break, Frank (Mr. Foreman) asks, "Is it time yet?"

"No," Angela smiles, "not yet."

Sometimes, after a weekend, Frank asks her, "Now?"

"No," Angela laughs, "not yet."

I love watching her so comfortable and secure about her body, so sure of herself, so secure about our support, so ready to be celebratory.

One day, Angela comes into my room during lunch. Frank and I are sitting at a table, eating. "NOW!" she beams. We jump up and give her a hug. We set a date for the ritual to take place at my house. Angela begins to use some of her time in her art class to make special invitations for this event.

Before I describe the ritual, I want to tell you about Angela when she was in the sixth grade. It was clear right away that she would be one of our outstanding writers. But it is her heart that I remember, her willingness to share everything about herself in class. Angela's father is a gay man, and she spent half her time in his family. I remember a photograph of her twelfth birthday party. Her father's partner had baked a wonderful, purple cake, and Angela brought a picture of herself with her father and her father's partner, happily grouped around this cake. She spent the other half of her time with her mother, her stepfather, her half-brother and half-sister. During her sixth grade year, her mother and step-father divorced, and her mother became involved with another woman.

"You think you have problems," Angela said one day. "BOTH my parents are gay." But it was always clear that Angela loved both her parents, that they both loved her, and that while this was an adjustment for Angela, it was certainly not a tragedy. Her mother eventually moved to Sonoma county, so Angela spent more time with her father.

That year we had the opportunity to enter a Bank of America essay contest. The assignment was to write about someone you admire, and Angela wrote a beautiful essay about her mother. As we read these essays in class, Angela shared that she wasn't sure whether or not to say anything about her mother's sexual identity. She wanted to, because that was a part of who her mother was. But she also wanted to win the essay, and she didn't think that Bank of America would award her for writing about a bisexual mother. She shared this dilemna with the class, and I remember that they took it seriously. In the end, she didn't say anything about her mother's sexual identification, but she felt bad about it. She won first prize.

I also remember that we wrote rough drafts and responded to them in class, and that the final drafts were due the next day, when I had to submit them to the contest. Angela was going skiing with her Dad and wouldn't be coming to school the next day, so I drove to her house early in the morning to pick up her final paper so I could submit it with the others. When she won, I remember feeling glad that I had made this extra effort.

On the morning of Angela's ritual, I went to the flower market. It was March, and I bought yellow tulips, purple irises, and white baby's breath. It was a time when I was between roommates, so I had an empty room in my house available for this ritual. I put the flowers in vases, and began to collect symbols from around my house. On the floor I put a colorful, embroidered cloth from India, and a bright *khanga* (a brightly colored cloth worn by women) from Kenya. I placed two red candles, some incense, a Snake Goddess from Crete, a female Buddhasatva from India, a Masaii fertility doll from Kenya, some water from the Ganges River, a Greek bowl with ocean water, a seashell, and some stones in the center of the room. I added a small Pomo wedding basket, a Mexican angel candle, and a bottle of red wine. (Now when I look back at the pictures, I see that there was also a hearth broom in the room, although I didn't plan that.)

Angela arrived with her mother and her mother's partner. Her father came alone. As Angela's friends arrived, I was touched by their attire—they wore hats, long gloves, and long skirts. I, too, had on a long dress. We sat around the center, and I asked everyone to put something they had brought in the middle of the circle and to tell about it. Angela brought her grandmothers' photographs. Frank brought his grandfather's gold watch and some red Focaccia bread. The girls had brought flowers: narcissus, calla lilies, red tulips, and pink roses.

I told Frank and Angela's father that I had never done rituals with men before, and I didn't know how to do them with men, although I was really glad they were there and I wanted them to feel welcome. I explained that I would be conducting this ritual as if we were all women, so I asked them to get in touch with the female side of them for this ritual, or to pass when we went around the circle, whichever they felt most comfortable with.

Angela lit the candles, and we honored the East, the South, the West and the North, and the elements of air, fire, water, and earth. We talked about menstruation as a gift of life. We passed a cup of wine around the circle, each of us saying as we drank, "We are women who bleed but are not wounded. We bleed to bring life into the world."

We passed around a basket with beads in it. I asked everyone to take a bead, to hold it in her hand, and to think of it as a seed. "As it warms in your hand," I said, "think of a gift that you want to give to Angela. Imagine that gift going into the bead/seed." Then, we passed around a needle and thread. As each participant told Angela the gift they imagined for her, she would string the bead onto the thread. Angela received gifts like strength, humor, happiness. When it was my turn, I wished for her strong and healthy sexual ecstasy. "But not yet!" her father blurted out, and we all laughed. When the circle was complete, we gave Angela this beaded necklace, full of the love and best wishes of her friends and family.

Angela's mother read her a poem she had written for the occassion. This poem was a perfect closing for the ritual:

FOR ANGELA AT PUBERTY

I wish I had something
to pass on to you now—
a gold watch
a diamond ring—
something permanent and lasting.
But I have none of these
for you, never have had
such things as these
for you.
When I look back
at our lives together
I see the many homes
and people
we have shared

since your birth—
practically on the road.
And then I see in each place
with whomever we shared it
the comfort, warmth, security
of love.
I see many, many good times—
in country places
city flats
on the road.
All those birthday parties—
two a year for the first six
or so
in city parks and sandy beaches—
always lots of friends around.
In all the moves
the comings and goings of people
into and out of your life
I remember only once
(aside from the big move of your daddy)
when you were not ready.
You were four, and the landlord came
to our little house on Duncan Street
claiming for his own new place
the furniture his grandmother had left
years ago.
"Mommy!" you wailed.
"He's taking our refrigerator,
he's taking our couch!"
"It's okay, honey.
He thinks it's his stuff.
We'll get another fridge, another couch."
What am I passing on to you?
The impermanence of things—
their value only as tools
when we need them.
The changing landscape of where
and with whom
you live according to what's right
and best—or simply necessary—
at the time.
I pass on to you
flow.

This menstrual flow
we are celebrating today—
from woman to woman—
that I am—
that you are.
The beautiful, unique, miraculous
flow
of your Angela spirit.
Angela—Angelita
Angel mine.
Angela who, in her babyhood,
comforted all who held her.
Angela in her toddler self—
always coming back from
some nice old man on the street
with a hot quarter clutched tightly
in her fist.
(A casual blessing from a stranger.)
Angela as a little girl
dancing across the street to school
in a fairy costume or tap shoes!
Angela, the serious ballerina from age five onward
pudgy arms raised in grace
as she pirouetted around the living room—
whatever living room you found yourself in.
My Angela
Bill's Angela
Erin and Jeff's Angela
her many grandparents' Angela
her step-parents' Angela
her friends' and teachers' and roomates' Angela.
An Angela who always flowed outward to us all.
Now today
I pass on to you
that this flow is good.
Better than good—
it's WONDERFUL!
It is your blessing
from me to me.
Thank you, daughter mine.

All of us were teary when Angela's mother finished her poem. It was time to celebrate. We ate bread and cheese and drank water and wine. The ritual became a party, and then the other adults had to leave. The girls wanted to stay. "You said you were going to do a guided fantasy," they said. "Yes, I was, but the poem was so perfect it deserved to have the party right afterwards," I said. The girls decide to stay and finish this part, the other adults leave.

It is suddenly very cold in the room. I go to my bedroom to find shawls for everyone. Rosie is retrieving her sweater from my bed, and she looks sad. I ask her what is wrong. "I just had my thirteenth birthday," she says. "I wish my mother had done something like this for me."

I put my arm around her. "She would have, if she knew about it," I tell her. "This ritual is really for all of us, Rosie. It is specifically for Angela, but it is really about all of us. Don't be hard on your mother for not thinking of this. Women have been taught for many many generations now not to celebrate their womanhood."

We return to the "ritual room" with warm shawls and sweaters, and everyone bundles up. I turn on the tape player with the tape that will take us on an internal journey. We make ourselves comfortable and close our eyes. We mentally go down a spiral staircase into deep relaxation, until we enter a special room at the bottom of the staircase. Behind a door someone is waiting for us. We open the door, and greet that person, who then gives us a gift to bring back. In my case I meet my grandmother, who gives me her brown, plastic, rectangular hearing device, the one that the wires from her ears plugged into, the one she kept deep in her bosom, between her breasts. As a child, I used to climb on her slippery lap, and speak directly into her bosom, knowing that it was like speaking into her ear. Sometimes this hearing aid would cackle and crack with static.

The voice on the tape guides us back up the spiral staircase, until we open our eyes and re-enter the circle. Eve, sitting on my left, begins to cry. But it feels like a healthy, good cry, so I am not worried. I am glad the other adults are not there, however, as I think it would worry them. I put my arm around Eve's shoulders to comfort her. "Let's go around the circle, and talk about what happened to us on this journey," I say. "Eve, you can go last, or if you don't want to talk about what happened, you may pass."

The girls begin to tell their stories. I can't remember them all now, but I remember being astounded at how powerful they all were. One received a turquoise ring. One received a silver mirror. One received a white rose. One received a seashell. If I had been Jung, planning it all out ahead of time, it couldn't have turned out any better. When we get to Eve, her crying had stopped, and she had been listening to the stories of the others. She told us that she met her grandfather behind the door. This grandfather died just a few weeks ago. Eve didn't go to the hospital to see him before he died, and she felt bad about this. She was surprised to see him on this journey. His words to her were powerful. He told her how much he loved her, how proud he was of her, how she should always remember that she comes from a strong and loving family, but that she should also always be herself, and listen to herself. He gives her a picture of himself as a young man.

When Eve tells us this story, she cries again. "Do you have this photograph of your grandfather in real life?" I ask. "Yes," she says. "I really have this picture. It is a real gift, not just a gift of my imagination." We are each touched by Eve's story. The ritual feels perfect.

The girls gather up their things before I drive them home. They thank me. "If you want to give me a present," I say, "write about this and give me a copy." While all of them intend to, only one of them does.

I describe the ritual to my friend Valorie. Each girl got a lovely, feminine gift, I say, except me. I tell her the story of my grandmother's brown plastic hearing aid, stuffed into her bosom. "Oh, Judy," she says. "You got that gift because you know how to listen with your heart."

This last Christmas Angela came over for dinner. She is a sophomore in college now, in Minnesota. We had a long conversation, catching up on news. She talked about her anger and fear when her father told her he was HIV positive. She talked about her pride in her mother. "I had to go to college to discover my mother as a scholar," she said. She talked about wanting to be a teacher, at least for a few years, and how distressed her father is about this decision. "It will look bad on your resume," he told her.

"What kind of a teacher do you want to be?" I ask Angela.

"I want to do what you do," she says, and I think to myself, remember this moment.

losing it:
notes about field trips

IT IS A beautiful, sunny, warm afternoon, perfect for driving across the Golden Gate Bridge. My friend, Jeanne Gallo, has taken her sixth grade class on a two-day camping trip. She is camped at Kirby Cove, in the Golden Gate Headlands, a redwood grove right on the Pacific Ocean just west of the Golden Gate Bridge. My colleague Frank and I have been invited to join them for dinner, and as we drive over the bridge, I am relishing the fact that this is not MY field trip. I have taken my students on this camping trip many times, and it feels luxurious to be driving over the bridge, instead of walking forty or fifty students across the bridge after having gotten up at five o'clock in the morning to load my car with two days' worth of food, driving it across the bridge and parking it, then meeting a friend to drive me back to school before eight. This time, it is Jeanne's turn. I get to just enjoy the company of the students, the view of the ocean, the smell of hot dogs on an open fire.

When we arrive the scene is peaceful. Students are lolling on the beach, or playing volleyball, or hiking in the hills. Jeanne is alone—the teacher with whom she planned this camping trip told her at the last minute that he had a class at state college that night, so he might as well just sleep at home. This leaves Jeanne alone with thirty students and no car in case of an emergency. Frank and I decide to stay until bedtime, in case any students need a ride. (I have taken many sick children home over the years, and I've visited the emergency room more than once—I know that a car is essential.)

While the students are having a good time, Jeanne and Frank and I sit at a picnic table in the sun and begin to tell field trip stories. I strongly believe in taking children out of the classroom, and over the years I have taken many field trips, and something has almost always gone wrong. I tell about the time when I was a very young teacher and I believed my students from Hunter's Point would benefit from a day spent at San Francisco State College. I arranged for the Black Students' Union to give them a guided tour. On the way home, they set fire to the back seat of the bus. The bus driver pulled over to the side of the road and yelled at me, "Lady, can't you control those kids?"

I did the only thing I could think of doing: I put my hand on my hip, mustered what dignity I could, and replied, "Does it look like I can control these kids?" He threw us off the bus. I took this same class to visit the *Sun Reporter*, the only Black-owned and run newspaper in San Francisco. While waiting at a bus stop to transfer, a candy truck pulled up in front of a drugstore and the driver LEFT ITS BACK DOOR UP WHILE HE DELIVERED SEVERAL BOXES OF CANDY INSIDE! My students saw this as an open invitation, and I became octopus-like, using my arms, legs, head and body to block grabs for Hersheys, Snickers, Reese's Peanut Butter Cups, Milky Ways and Oh Henrys. It was about this time that I began wearing disguises on field trips: dark glasses, hats, bulky coats.

When I changed schools, field trips continued to be problematic. There was the time I had to write a note home explaining why one of my students had whiskey sloshed all over his sweatshirt. We were on a crowded bus, and when it lurched to one side, a drunk man who was trying to drink out of a bottle in a paper bag missed, and the contents spilled onto my student's sweatshirt hood. "Please excuse the smell on Jimmy's sweatshirt . . ."

Or the time that Kathie and I were walking sixty students to the streetcar stop after an afternoon of ice-skating. When I rounded the corner, sixty students were running around in circles, laughing, covering their eyes, totally confused. It was as if the God Pan himself had appeared among them. It took a moment to figure out what was going on, but I soon saw that across the street in a second floor motel picture window, a very fat naked man was waving a bottle of spirits, laughing, and moving his hips so that his penis flopped back and forth. I walked calmly into the motel office to report this offense, and asked the proprietor to call the police. When the man saw me heading towards the office, he closed the drapes.

The chaos this caused was no worse than the time I was walking a sixth grade class to the bus stop after attending a play at University High School. On this occasion, the students also suddenly started running around, screaming, and laughing—only this time it was because of two dogs mating. For those of you who are not teachers, or for those of you who do not teach sixth grade, believe me, you have not lived until you walk 36 sixth graders past two dogs mating.

While Jeanne and Frank and I are visiting, her students organize and cook dinner, serving us at our picnic table. I tell Jeanne about the time some teachers reserved this campground only to discover once they were here that the other part of it had been reserved by a movie company making a "B" movie. The movie was about a war between Arabs and Africans. The scene they were filming was a night scene, where the Arabs landed on the beach and the Africans defended it. The beach, the hills, and the bunkers were wired with fake explosives. Those and the strong lights kept everyone up all night. The only good thing was that a baseball hero who was starring in the movie came and had hot dogs with the kids. Fortunately for me, this was someone else's field trip. I just visited to give moral support, got to drive home and sleep in my own bed, and heard the horror stories later.

I tell about the time that I had forty students walking to the theater from the bus stop, when three strangers singled out one of my male students and practiced Kung Fu on him and then ran away. And the time I arranged to spend a whole day at the zoo with some other teachers and our classes, but we were sent home by the police when some students broke all the phones to steal change. Or the time I took eighth graders on a bus to Sacramento, stopping at the Milk Farm for a meal on the way home. It wasn't until the Milk Farm sent a large bill to my school that I realized that the students had helped themselves to the large stack of milk chocolate bars displayed by the cash register.

On a recent trip to the Oakland Museum to see a display of African-American quilts, several students got lost. Two parents had come along to help, and we boarded two different subway cars. About six girls who were in the car next to mine decided to take advantage of my not being there, and began walking from one car to the other, which they are not supposed to do. When we came to our stop, they didn't know it was time to get off since they were in a different car. As I was counting noses in the station, I saw the six of them pressed up against the glass in the last car, looking worried and distraught as the train pulled out.

The rest of the kids were very upset. "What will happen to them? What should they do? Will they get in trouble?" I calmed them down. "You wait here," I told them. "The girls will have sense enough to get off at the next station and come back. I'll go upstairs and speak to the station master." I did so, and explained the problem. She was kind enough to phone ahead to the next station and ask the security people to meet my students and make sure they returned by the next train. I rejoined the class, confident that the girls would show up soon. But several trains later I began to worry. I revisited the station master, and she phoned ahead to check with security. They reported that the girls had not disembarked. So she got on the paging system and announced, "Will Ms. Logan's students please call 214. Will Ms. Logan's students please call 214." I returned to the train platform downstairs to see the rest of my class running around wildly looking for a phone.

"Not you," I explained to them. "We want the LOST students to call."

Shortly thereafter, a train arrived with the lost girls. I was relieved as I had begun to really worry. So had they. Two of them were crying and needed to be held, the other four were clearly shaken. We all sat down in a quiet place to hear what had happened.

Realizing they had missed our stop, the girls explained that they traveled to the front of the train until they reached the conductor and told him their plight. He advised them to wait two stops before getting off, as the next station had a complicated way of trying to return, whereas the second station was quite simple. They stayed together and followed his advice, but it took awhile as the second station was quite far away. I asked them what they had learned from this experience, and they came up with all the right answers ("Stay with the group, stay together"). I complimented them on making good decisions and reassured them that they were now fine.

Jeanne's class is building a campfire and getting ready for entertainment. It continues to be the perfect field trip. I go on to tell Jeanne my two favorite field trip stories.

Once, I allowed a few sixth graders to accompany a Shakespeare class to an outdoor performance of *Macbeth*. My seventh and eighth grade class had read and studied the play, but the sixth graders had not. They were eager to go however, and they were good students, so I let them. The performance was terrible—one of the worst I have ever seen. Returning from the theater, one sixth grader walked beside me in silence. I could feel her puzzling things out. Finally she said, "Which one was Macbeth?"

Another time, I had taken a large group of students to see a matinee performance of Chekov's *The Cherry Orchard*. The performance was magnificent, and the students were moved. One particularly sensitive sixth grader walked beside me silently for some time, and again, I could feel her puzzling things out. "That was so sad," she said.

"Yes," I reply.

"I mean it was REALLY sad," she said again. "Sadder than E.T."

Because of this experience, she chose Anton Chekov over Steven Spielberg. Who says field trips aren't worth it?

Night has fallen and nobody is sick, nobody is homesick, nobody is misbehaving. Frank and I can leave Jeanne and her class to sleep out under the stars, with the sound of the ocean in their ears. We congratulate her again on having arranged the perfect field trip, hug her goodbye, and begin the slow winding drive up the dirt road to the top of the hill. When we get to the top, a ranger's truck pulls over and stops us. "Are you with the school group camped out below?" they ask us.

"Unofficially we are, officers. Why, is there a problem?"

"Yes, Ma'am, there is a problem. We have to get those kids out of there right away. There's just been a big earthquake in Alaska and there's a tsunami heading this way. We may have twenty-foot tidal waves. We have orders to clear all coastal areas. I want those kids on high ground in fifteen minutes. Tell them to leave their food, sleeping bags and other equipment behind, and to just hike immediately to high ground."

Frank drives down to tell Jeanne and the kids. I hike to a pay phone by the bridge to call the principal and ask him to call teachers to volunteer to drive the kids home. It is two hours before everyone is safely delivered home. (By the way, the tsunami never came.) So much for the perfect field trip.

some middle school strategies for black history month

I HAVE BEEN struggling for many years now with how to make curriculum multicultural and gender-inclusive, and each year I learn something new. While I am uncomfortable with isolating February as Black History Month, or March as Women's History Month, I find that it provides me with a focus and community support for particular projects. For example, my class researches and writes essays on women from history in order to participate in the NOW essay contest. Because these essays have to be submitted in mid-December, however—even though the reception for the winners doesn't take place until Women's History Month—we begin working on them in the fall, and thus we focus on them for more than half the year.

In February I especially focus on Black History. I have asked students to choose one African American person, to research his or her life completely, and to come to class as that person in order to tell the story of his or her life. Students are encouraged to use photographs, illustrations, costumes, props, music, drama and/or video tapes in order to make the person's life real to the class. I provide a list to choose from which students can add to. Last year I noticed that while all the boys chose males to report on, two girls chose to be males (Gordon Parks and Martin Luther King). I was uncomfortable that females chose to be males while males did not choose to be females. I began to wonder what I could do to help all students feel comfortable exploring both male and female lives. So this year I modified the assignment so that each student was required to do two reports—one on a male, and one on a female.

Initially, I was surprised that not one student objected to doing two reports, or to "becoming" a person of the opposite gender. All of their questions were about whether or not they could extend my list. (By this time in the semester they know that I like them to collaborate and alter my assignments.) But as they raised their hands to say, "Could I be Janet

Jackson?" or "Could I be Bill Cosby?" I realized that they saw this assignment as an opportunity to become one of their heroes from the sports or
entertainment field. Instead of saying no, I said yes to each request. Then
I asked them to look at the list they had constructed on the board. We had
only athletes and entertainers. "This is a great list," I said, "but it is not Black
History. In fact, I would be embarassed to have this list leave the room as
our concept of Black History, because, even though these great people are
an integral part of Black History, they are not the whole picture. How would
you feel if I said we were going to study White History and then we only
studied movie stars and sports heroes? I know that you don't know yet about
the people I put on the list, but trust me, they have interesting lives, and
you will like getting to know them." Slowly hands were raised and students
began trading their heroes for names unknown. By not saying no to them
in the first place, we as a class were allowed to confront our limited percep-
tions of Black contributions to society.

Once I had accomplished the above, my job as teacher for the next
several weeks was to bring a lot of material to class. We watched the PBS
series *Getting to Know Me*, ten half-hour dramatic programs on a Black
family, each of which celebrates some aspect of Black culture. We watched
segments of programs on Black History. We read poems, listened to music,
read stories. Each day I would say, "Class, who in this class is Alice Walker?"
Pauline would raise her hand. "Pauline, you wrote the poems I will be
reading today." And Pauline would smile. Or, "Who in this class is Malcolm
X?" David would raise his hand. "David, you will be making a very important speech in today's video, watch carefully." And he would. Or, "Who is
Bernice Reagan Johnson? . . . Simon, you wrote this music, and you will see
yourself in this tape." Of course, I also provided them with library time so
they could research independently.

The last week of the month I get to sit in the back of the room and watch
some amazing presentations. Some students choose to do both their male
and female roles in succession, some do just one, then wait until later for
their second presentation. Their work delights me. Emma comes in one
morning before homeroom and hands me a white florist's box, and asks me
to keep it in the refrigerator for her. Later in class, she carefully, tenderly
pins a white gardenia in her hair before beginning her report as Billie
Holiday. Her friend pushes the on and off button on the tape recorder so
that Billie's music is part of her report.

Bret comes to school in a black suit, dons black horned-rimmed glasses,
and is Langston Hughes. He then goes behind the file cabinets, and a few
minutes later reappears as Sojourner Truth, wearing a large housedress and
a cotton scarf on his head. Akiko has taken a large poster board and cut a
hole out of the center, just large enough to stick her face through. Around
her face she has drawn hair, and a small-scale but muscular body in boxing
trunks, with gloves on, in a ring. She tells her story as Muhammad Ali. Then,

she turns the poster board around and pokes her face through again. This time she has drawn an elaborate hairdo, a shimmering gown. She holds a microphone as she stands on stage, and she tells us her story as Tina Turner. Paul Robeson shows us a part of a film he made, and we listen to him sing. Jesse Jackson and Shirley Chisholm share their campaign speeches. Mary McLeod Bethune tells us about her struggles to begin her school, and Sara Lawrence Lightfoot shares her educational philosophies. Students refer to 3x5 cards, but for the most part they seem to have internalized these stories and tell them from memory.

Emma, this time as Joe Louis, wears a purple silk robe on the back of which she has taped the words, BROWN POWER. When she gets to the moment in her story when she is fighting for the heavyweight championship of the world, she says, "But wait, it was such an exciting moment, I can't possibly describe it to you. Let me show you . . . " and she slips a tape into the video machine.

Pauline climbs up on my tall teacher's stool. She wraps herself in a large purple shawl. "Dear God," she begins. "My name is Alice Walker . . . "

Sometimes I interview the students while they are in character. "So, James Meredith, there you were with all those TV cameras, national guardsmen, hostile crowds, how did you feel as you walked down that street toward school?" The students reply in character. "I was scared, but I was determined. And I felt proud. I knew what I was doing was dangerous, but I knew I needed that education and I wasn't going to let anything stop me. I had a lot of support from my friends and community." Sometimes a student will say something like, "Well, Ms. Logan, this happened a long time ago, and I can't remember right now how I felt, but I'll look at my journals tonight and give it some thought, and get back to you tomorrow."

A nice moment in this assignment: Lena, as Zora Neale Hurston, to Bret, as Langston Hughes, "Bret, I know you!" And she tells us about how Zora's and Langston's lives intersected. Other students also begin telling how they knew or admired other students' characters. They say things like, "I found you in my life too!" We have moved from individual presentations to an exploration of how these people were related in time and space.

Another nice moment: Many weeks later, the class is on a field trip to the Oakland Museum to see a show called, "Strength and Diversity: A History of the Japanese American Woman." Some parents have volunteered to accompany us, and as we walk towards the museum, Bret's mother says, "Judy, I want to tell you how much I appreciate your social studies program. Not long ago, Bret had some friends over from another school, and I overheard them talking about their classes. Bret had a wealth of information about women and about minorities. And his friends didn't know anything about the people he was talking about. I'm really grateful that he has your class."

the NOW contests

IT IS 1986 and I see a flier telling me that the San Francisco branch of the National Organization of Women is sponsoring an essay contest in middle schools for Women's History Month. The essay must be about a famous woman in history, it must be thoroughly researched and well-written, it must be typed on only one side of the paper with the names of the writer, the school, and the teacher on the back of each page, so that the contest can be judged anonymously. Essay prizes are $75, $50, and $25 for first, second and third place; ribbons and certificates will also be awarded.

My sixth-grade students have done a lot of work on women in history, so we decide to enter the contest. Each sixth grader writes an essay as part of a class assignment. I announce the contest to my seventh and eighth graders, and some of them choose to enter as well. We read each other's essays and decide as a class which ones to submit. We are supposed to turn in the "top three" from each class, but since I have these students for three periods a day for three subjects, we turn in nine essays to represent us.

Some time later I receive a phone call telling me that we have won first and second place for sixth grade, second place for seventh grade, and an honorable mention. Hallie has won for writing about Mother Jones, Emma for Laura Ingalls Wilder, Vanessa for Virginia Woolf, and Maria for Alice Walker. I have a great time phoning the students at home, putting their names in the daily school bulletin, announcing the results in class, and later attending a reception sponsored by NOW at which each winner reads her essay aloud and receives her award. Some days later I receive a note from Hallie's mother: "Three winners in one class? You're the one who deserves the prize. What you have done for both my kids' writing is a gift I'll never forget." I still have this note on my dresser.

One day Maria comes to class and tells me she has attended the graduation ceremonies at her elementary school. "And guess who was there?" she asks me. "Alice Walker!" I am delighted as Maria describes how she introduced herself to Alice Walker as someone who had recently won an essay contest by writing about her.

The next year I announce to the sixth graders that we will again be entering the contest. "I expect some of you will win this year," I say. They become anxious and angry, and say things like: "How unfair! What if we don't win? This is too much pressure," and so on. "Oh, it's okay if you don't win," I say, "but ever since I have been teaching sixth grade I have entered my students' writing in some essay contest or another, and we have always had a winner. This class is full of fine writers. It's okay if we don't win this year, but I will be surprised if we don't. Anyway, the contest is a long way off. We will learn a lot about writing between now and then."

Again, the NOW contest is a mandatory assignment for sixth graders, an optional one for seventh and eighth graders. I am again delighted to receive a phone call telling me that Hallie has won first place for her seventh-grade essay on Sarah Winnemucca, Janet second place for her sixth-grade essay on Helen Keller, Amelia seventh-grade second place for Clara Barton, and there are two honorable mentions: Rain for her essay on Winnie Mandela, and Noah for his essay on his grandmother, Ruth Asawa. I am delighted that Noah, our first male winner, won with our first essay about a family member. Again we attend the reception. I ask Hallie what she will do with her $75. "It is my sister Rosie's birthday this month," she says, "and I am going to donate it to the Nicaraguan Ambulance Fund in her name."

The following year I give my we-have-always-won-a-contest speech. Again the students become angry and accuse me of being unfair, again I reassure them that it is okay if we don't win. In doing this, I not only challenge them, but also deflect the competition that they might feel with each other onto the past classes. This way, if only one person wins in the contest, that person is winning for the whole class and places the class in the we-have-always-won-a-contest hall of fame. But not just one person wins the contest: This year the phone call tells me we have won first place in sixth, seventh, and eighth grades; second place in sixth and seventh grades; third place in sixth and seventh grades; and we have five honorable mentions. "Isn't anyone else entering the contest?" I ask meekly. "Oh yes," the caller assures me, "we had more entries than ever this year. Almost all middle schools in the city are participating, as well as some private schools."

My students are thrilled when I make the announcement. This year they have written about Margaret Sanger, Emma Goldman, Winnie Mandela, Dian Fossey, Hildegarde of Bingen, Anne Frank, Jane Addams, Lucretia Mott, and Joan Baez. Hallie, as an eighth grader, has won first place again for an essay on Mother Teresa. This year she didn't want to write an essay (which is optional for eighth graders). She told me she was very busy, and I think she is a little embarrassed that she won first place two years in a row. But I push her into it, keeping her in at lunch just a day before the essays are due, insisting that she write something, even if it is only a rough draft. "I wanted to do Mother Teresa," Hallie tells me, "but I haven't had time to do any research." By this time, Hallie and I are good friends. I feel comfortable pushing her a little, and she takes it well. I pop a video on Mother Teresa into the VCR for her to watch. "You'll do better with a rough draft than most people would with hours of work," I tell her. "It would be a shame not to enter this year when you have done so well in the past."

So I am particularly happy with her first prize award. So are the NOW people. At the reception they call Hallie up specially to give her flowers. They also call me up specially, and give me flowers. I say a few words thanking them for this opportunity to write about women, and predict that some day we will be writing about Hallie.

The NOW group also asks me to come to their meeting and talk about feminist curriculum, since I must be doing something right in order to have all these kids writing winning essays. I have a good time speaking to their group. They meet in the Women's Building on 18th Street, which used to be Dovre Hall and housed the Norwegian Club. As a child I spent a lot of time there at Christmas parties, weddings, and family reunions, as my grandparents were Norwegian immigrants. The room where NOW meets, where I stand and talk about my classes, is the room where my parents held their wedding reception, where my grandparents had their Golden Anniversary party. I feel a sense of personal history that pleases me.

For my presentation, I explain how I incorporate women's history and multicultural themes into my classroom curriculum, I talk about Peggy McIntosh's Phase Theory, and I show slides of some of my students' work. The NOW group decides to change its policy and allow students to write about non-famous people in history, like mothers and grandmothers.

*   *   *   *

In 1989 we again win first place for sixth, seventh and eighth grades, second place for sixth, seventh, and eighth grades, and third place for sixth and seventh grades. We have also five honorable mentions. Even I'm impressed. Students have written about family, friends and teachers, as well as Cyndi Lauper, Joan Baez, Rosa Parks, Shirley Chisholm, Benazir Bhutto, and Dianne Feinstein, the mayor of San Francisco.

Ben has written a wonderful essay about his mother, who is a midwife, and his essay includes a summary of the history of midwifery. At the reception, he asks his mother to stand while he reads it aloud, and we all have a teary moment. Thea has written about the mayor. She sends a copy of her essay to the mayor's office. Later Thea receives a beautiful crystal vase from Dianne Feinstein, and she is able to meet Ms. Feinstein in person at a reception on nearby Treasure Island.

*   *   *   *

In 1990 I give my we-have-always-won-a-contest speech to my new sixth graders. Students gulp and protest as usual, and I give my same calm, reassuring it's-okay-if-we-don't-but-I'll-be-surprised reply. Again we win first place for sixth, seventh, and eighth grades. We win second place in sixth, seventh, and eighth grades. We win third place for sixth and seventh grades, and we get four honorable mentions. "Are you sure other people are entering this contest?" I ask my NOW friends. They tell me they had over 500 entries this year. My students have written about Elizabeth Gurley Flynn, Sylvia Plath, Michelle Cliff, Helen Caldicott, and Simone de Beauvoir, as well as aunts, teachers, mothers and grandmothers. Two of their essays are published in a San Francisco newspaper.

Rain has graduated from eighth grade and is a freshman in high school. Her mother sends me a note telling me that Rain just won an essay contest on Martin Luther King, and she is kind enough to send me a copy of the essay and a program from the awards ceremony along with the note. Rain entered this contest on her own, she tells me.

*   *   *   *

As a sixth grader, Shoshannah wrote her essay on Ann Richards, who had spoken at the 1988 Democratic convention. She didn't win a prize, although it was a great essay. Some of Shoshannah's family friends, who have a business greeting and escorting visiting dignitaries around San Francisco, remembered her essay and invited her to accompany them when Ann Richards came to San Francisco for a book signing party. Shoshannah got a copy of her essay from me and took it to the party where she had her picture taken as she presented Ann Richards with her essay. The next year Shoshannah was invited to the Inaugural Ball in Texas when Ann Richards became governor. I remember that Shoshannah wrote a wonderful piece in the sixth grade about her three heroes. They were Hallie, her classmate; Judy Logan (me), her teacher; and Ann Richards. I am thrilled that she was able to meet her third hero.

This year Shoshannah wins first place for her seventh grade essay on Janet Stafford, a neighbor, a pediatrician, and a family friend who is a wife and mother in an interracial marriage. In this essay she focuses on Janet's courageous battle with breast cancer, celebrates her survival instincts, and describes how Janet's battle with cancer helped her to see the children under her care at the hospital as survivors. When Shoshannah finishes reading her essay, she introduces Janet to the audience. It is another teary moment. After the NOW reception Shoshannah's mother takes Janet, Shoshannah and me to lunch. I learn that Janet was present at Shoshannah's birth.

Later that year Shoshannah's mother, Judith, discovers a lump in her breast. She calls me to tell me what is going on, when she is going for her biopsy, how she is feeling. Shoshannah comes in to see me one morning before school. "It was malignant," she says. "Oh shit," I blurt out without thinking. When I call Judith later, she says Shoshannah came home and said, "Mom, Ms. Logan never swears, but today when I told her she said 'Oh shit.'" We talk about her upcoming surgery, her chemotherapy, her radiation. I try to keep in close touch but Shoshannah seems calm and doesn't want to talk about it much. She just happens to begin writing about incredibly angry daughters and dying mothers for the writing club.

*   *   *   *

The next year I am going on sabbatical leave. "But what about the NOW essay contest?" the students ask. "Mr. Foreman will do the essay contest next year," I tell them. "If there is a winner from our school, I promise I will come home from wherever I am to attend the reception in March." When it is time for the contest, Frank puts a tremendous amount of energy into helping students choose topics, collecting the essays, submitting them, etc. In February he proudly calls me to tell me that our students have won first place in seventh and eighth grades, second place in seventh and eighth grades, third place in sixth and eighth grades, and four honorable mentions. I am thrilled; the students are thrilled. When it is time for the reception, my friend Nancy Letts happens to be presenting at a conference in San Francisco, and she takes time to attend the reception with me. This year, students have written about Eleanor Roosevelt, Indira Gandhi, Amelia Earhart, Georgia O'Keeffe, Mary McLeod Bethune, Imogen Cunningham, and Morgaine le Faye, as well as about parents, teachers, and grandmothers. But it is Shoshannah's essay on her mother that touches me most deeply. She titles it "A Will To Live," and it is a beautiful essay about her mother's life, including this last year's successful struggle with cancer. Nancy sits on one side of me and Frank sits on the other side of me and we all three quietly cry through the whole presentation.

*   *   *   *

This year in September when I return to teaching, I will say to my sixth graders, "Ever since I started teaching sixth grade we have had city-wide essay contest winners in this class. My classes have a reputation for winning contests." And the students will say, "That's really unfair to put that kind of pressure on us. How will we feel if we don't win a contest?" And I will say, "Oh, it's okay with me if we don't win, I don't expect this to go on forever . . . but I will be surprised if we don't, because we have such good writers in this class . . ."

Who knows what will happen?

notes about problems

HALLIE, WHO IS now a sophomore in high school, calls me. (Hallie is the student who won the NOW contest three years in a row for writing about Mother Jones, Sarah Winnemucca, and Mother Teresa. Her class projects usually focused on women and men of color.) She has been invited to a costume party for the first day of spring, and she wants to talk about symbols of spring. At the end of our conversation, I ask her how school is going. "Not so well, Judy," she says. "I just got a 2.6 on my report card."

I am really surprised, because Hallie is among the most obviously smart and creative students I have ever had, and I tell her so. "What is going on?" I ask, "you are a straight 'A' student."

"I've just stopped trying," she says. "It's really boring. In English we have been studying Fitzgerald forever. I guess I'm just tired of studying about the emotional problems of middle-aged white men. And my history class is worse. I mean, my history teacher actually skipped over all the chapters in our book that weren't about Europe."

*   *   *   *

Suzanne is our AV clerk. She does all the duplicating of class materials, types out all the bulletins, and orders all the movies, videos and audio tapes for us. Her office is in a far corner of the third floor, and it is the place where all teachers go when they need supplies, last minute lesson plans duplicated, hugs, candy, tissues to dry tears, and a sympathetic heart. It is a kind of human hearth that exists on the marginal edge of the school, and which could never exist next door to the principal's office. Feminist scholars could write a great article analyzing and contrasting Suzanne's office and the principal's office as marginal versus central politics.

One year, Suzanne had planned to go to Paris in the summer. But when we had lunch at a restaurant with her one day in early December, she said she couldn't go because she just didn't have the money to travel and also pay her rent since she was unemployed every summer. One teacher who was also going to be in Paris wanted to meet her at a famous restaurant for lunch. "If you purchase your ticket before December 10th," he told her, "it will only cost you $560." But Suzanne said she just couldn't afford it.

When we returned to school, my friend Kathie said to me, "You know, Judy, if we could just get ten people to donate fifty dollars, we could buy that ticket for Suzanne for Christmas."

"What a great idea," I said. "You and I will certainly donate, we only have to find eight more people." Kathie had a class just then, but I had time to run around the school and share this idea. I easily got more than eight people to contribute. The principal contributed immediately, and some people gave more than fifty dollars. The next day, I took checks to the bank and got 9 one-hundred dollar bills. Kathie and I made a big mural with a crowd of people waving good-bye on a piece of land labeled "San Francisco." In the air, a red-headed Suzanne looked out of an airplane window. In Paris, our friend Deborah, who used to teach at our school, was standing by the Eiffel Tower waving hello. We stapled an envelope labeled "cab fare" to the San Francisco part. It had $100 in it. We stapled an envelope labeled "airfare" to the plane. It had $600 in it. We stapled an envelope labeled "lunch money" near Paris. It had $200 in it. We invited everyone who had contributed to come to our classroom at the beginning of lunch. At lunchtime, I stopped by Suzanne's room and casually asked her to come to our classroom. She seemed surprised to see all these people in our room. I turned her around to look at the mural. "Merry Christmas, Suzanne," we said, and I shoved a chair under her just in time as she collapsed in shock. We all cried. It was one of those great *It's A Wonderful Life*/Jimmy Stewart/Donna Reed moments.

*   *   *   *

This year, while I was on sabbatical, Suzanne's job as AV clerk was cut in half: she could work for the teachers only two periods a day. The rest of her day she had to work as a secretary for a federal program in our school. Then the new principal decided she didn't want Suzanne so far away from the central office, so she decided to move her closer. Teachers protested, but the principal didn't change her mind. Suzanne decided to quit her job and move back to Texas, after twenty years of being at our school, rather than move downstairs by the central offices.

Teachers lost the only person in the school whose full time job it was to give them direct help. And, because of the person she was, Suzanne gave us love and emotional support as well, no small loss in an environment that doesn't treat teachers well. No more last minute help, no more hugs, no more safe place to go cry. Most of the teachers, myself included, were devastated by this loss.

After Suzanne left, the already overloaded vice principal spent an hour each morning duplicating teacher material. (This one hour was supposed to replace what it took Suzanne a whole day to do.) If teachers didn't get their materials in before eight o'clock, the work did not get done. The downtown office, gearing up for massive cuts in the budget, refused to refill Suzanne's position.

My friend Kathie told me that one day, while she was picking up some material she had had run off, two students from the Filipino bilingual program brought some work that Mr. P. wanted duplicated. The vice principal yelled at them, "I TOLD YOU YESTERDAY THIS WAS TOO MUCH WORK TO DO!" Before the students could leave, he grabbed the packet Mr. P had sent up to be copied and dumped it in the wastebasket.

I worry about how it will be, returning to school without Suzanne there.

*   *   *   *

Natis, the boy who made the wonderful enameled moon mobile in my *Moon, Moon* class, has been expelled from Reed College: He sat in at the President's office, protesting investments in South Africa, and refused to leave.

Cybelle, the girl who made the Moon Goddess costume, drops out of high school. But she continues her art work, and she has her own radio program on a local station.

Belinda, one of my outstanding writers, also drops out of high school. I don't hear this story until years later when I run into her on the street. She wrote an essay for her English class. The teacher gave it an "F" because it was too good. "I have never met a fourteen-year-old girl who could think," he writes, "and I don't think I've met one now. You must have copied this." She asks him to call her former teachers, but he refuses. Her mother comes to school and speaks to the counselor. Finally, she is given a "C." The next year, when her history teacher says that while he does not condone assassination, it was in a way a fortunate thing that Harvey Milk (a gay city supervisor) was killed with San Francisco Mayor George Moscone, because gay politics were becoming too powerful in San Francisco, Belinda decides high school is not for her. She works for a while, takes the equivalency exam when she is old enough, and enters college.

*   *   *   *

As part of a business/education partnership program, the Pacific Bell Telephone Company (or "Pac Bell") has adopted our school. One of their officers comes to a faculty meeting and is very upbeat about the possibilities of this partnership. "Think about what you need," he tells us. "The sky is the limit."

Now, during this time, I am involved in a three-year research project with the Center for Research on Writing at UC Berkeley. All of my sixth graders' writing is copied, sent to this center, and then mailed to the

University of London and to Kate Chapman's class in London. All of her class's writing is also shared with us. The idea behind this project is to give the students' work an expanded audience.

It takes weeks for the mail to go back and forth. There are five teachers from the Bay Area and five teachers in London involved in this project. All the other teachers, including Kate, have computers, modems, and software that enable them to communicate directly and immediately without using the mail service. I have only computers in my classroom, but the center offers me software and a modem. All I need is a phone, and then Kate and I and our students can avoid all the mail expense and delay.

Since the sky is the limit, and since our school has just been adopted by a telephone company, it makes sense to me to ask Pac Bell for a telephone. I write a letter in September to the man in charge of the partnership program. I explain how my students can write a letter, a story, or a report, and it could be read by their writing partners in London the very next day, if only I had a telephone.

I never hear from him. My principal hears from him, however, and comes to explain to me that there are overseas communication laws, and that Pac Bell cannot possibly grant me an overseas connection. No problem, I tell him enthusiastically. The center at UC Berkeley already has the overseas connection. I just need to connect with the center, and they will send my work on to Kate.

I don't hear anything for a long time. When I finally approach the principal again, he tells me that everyone is worried about being unfair. "We don't want to give one teacher something that will make another teacher feel bad," he says.

"But I am the only teacher in the school involved in this project," I say. "I go to Berkeley once a month for meetings. I have student researchers and observers in my classroom frequently. It involves a lot of extra work. I don't get paid for this—couldn't I at least get a phone? If other teachers complain, you could explain that it is because I am part of this research project."

"What we're going to do," he tells me, "is we are going to set up a committee. This committee will begin meeting after Christmas vacation, and we are going to design a form for teachers to fill out so they can request things from Pac Bell. "

"But I already have my request," I say. "I already know what I want." "Fine," he says. "When the form comes out, you can fill it out." "But that will be February," I say. "School is over in June. How long will it take after the form is filled out?"

At Christmas time, Pac Bell gives every child in our school candy canes, pens, and pads of paper. Each teacher gets a bottle of wine.

Some teachers take their classes to Pac Bell and get tours of the plant and great lunches. Bigwigs from Pac Bell come to tour our school, and I love it when they come to my class. "Oh, class," I say, "here are the people from the telephone company who are going to help us get our phone!" We explain our research project and the history of our request. Pretty soon they take my classroom off the guided tour.

I never get the phone. Sometimes I laugh about this. Pac Bell adopted our school and the sky was the limit and I couldn't get a phone, ha ha.

Sometimes I drive around in my car and scream.

*   *   *   *

After their first five days at Lick Wilmerding, a private high school in San Francisco, Beverly, Gail and Ellen return to visit and tell me and my colleague, Frank, sternly, "You taught us wrong." Frank and I sit down with them to listen to their complaints. "Our teachers begin class by going around the room and asking questions like, what is the capital city of some place, or what date did something or other happen. The kids from private schools know all these answers, and we don't."

"Hmmmmm," I say, "I am sorry that is happening to you. I can imagine how it must feel, but you know a lot more than you think you know right now. Your time at here has not been spent just memorizing facts. You are all very sophisticated thinkers, your creative selves are alive and well, you are each skilled writers. You express yourselves brilliantly. My hunch is that in six weeks you will be the top students in the class. It will be much easier for you to catch up and memorize facts than it will be for the other students to learn how to think and express themselves well. When it is time to write essays, analyze literature, or discuss ideas, you three will excel, I'm sure. Please come back in six weeks and let me know what happens."

But it doesn't take six weeks. At our open house in the beginning of October, Ellen says sheepishly, "You were right. Now we're getting A's. I'm sorry we said those things to you."

Last fall I visited Ellen at Harvard, where she is a freshman. Together we attended a panel discussion led by Peggy McIntosh called "The Female Student at Harvard." I was shocked to hear story after story of sexual harassment. I worry that Ellen's middle school years might have been her last opportunity to study in a non-hierarchical, safe setting where women's and people of color's experiences were often central in the curriculum.

*   *   *   *

During a student-of-the-week interview, when it is time for the students to ask questions, Jody makes an unkind remark about the student being interviewed: She teases him about being gay. It is the third or fourth time that I have had to speak to her about making comments in class about people's sexual identity. I tell her to go to the counseling office. After class, I go to the counseling office only to find that she never went there—she just went on to her next class. When I explain the problem to her counselor, he decides to send her home to return with a parent. This is a Friday. On

Monday morning, someone comes into a meeting I'm in at eight o'clock to tell me that Jody's mother is waiting in my room. I go to see her. Jody's mother is treasurer of the PTA, I have met her many times, I consider her a friend. But when I get to my room, I see that she is furious with me. "I can't believe that I have had to get up out of a sick bed and come to school because you have a problem with my child calling other people faggots," she said. "I have adolescents hanging around my house all the time, and they are always calling each other gay and teasing each other. If you don't know this about adolescents, you have no business teaching this age." She stops yelling and starts crying. I get the tissues. Jody is having a good time watching this interaction between her mother and her teacher.

"First of all," I say, "I didn't send Jody home, her counselor did. I sent her to the office and she never went there, so that is why her counselor requested your presence today. Second, I don't have a say in what your daughter or her friends do in your home, but in this class it is not okay to tease people about being homosexual, or to use it as a putdown."

Jody's mother becomes furious. Sometimes she yells at me, sometimes she cries. She looks as though she could hit me. My friend Kathie, who shares the classroom with me, is at the other end of the room pacing back and forth, trying to figure out how to help me. This parent is hysterical and her daughter is having a great time watching. The parent says, "I see all this material about women, I know you teach about women, I think you have a very serious personal problem. I think you are taking what my daughter said very personally, and I think you are punishing her for your own problems. You have no business teaching."

"So," I say, "are you saying that you think I am a lesbian?"

"I didn't say that," she sniffs.

"Look," I say. "San Francisco has a written policy. We do not allow racial slurs, ethnic slurs, or homophobic slurs in the classroom. It is as simple as that. I consider sexual slurs to be as serious as racial slurs. But I know you are feeling sick today [several times during her ranting she has mentioned having the flu], why don't you go home and reschedule an appointment with the counselor at another time when you are feeling better?" She finally leaves, looking like she might slug me up to the last minute. First I go to the bathroom and cry. Kathie comes to comfort me.

"What a horrible experience," she says, "you didn't need this to start your day." Then I go to find the principal, so he will get Jody and speak to her before she gleefully reports her mother's accusations to the whole class. He does. Eventually she tells everyone anyway, but at least I get a little time before I have to deal with that problem.

A week or so later, Jody's mother makes an appointment with the counselor. It is my birthday. I tell the counselor that it is my birthday. "For a present," I ask, "don't make me sit through a meeting with Jody's mother." "Don't worry, I'll handle it, happy birthday," he tells me. Later, he says that she began the meeting by saying, "I owe Ms. Logan an apology." Well, she got that right, I tell him, and I thank him. He read her the city rule about slurs. (By this time, her daughter is also in trouble for carving her initials in a school violin.) Jody's mother finally realizes that sexual putdowns are not okay just because many adolescents participate in them. Our job as parents and teachers is to correct that behavior.

Several weeks later I deliver something to the main office, and Jody's mother is there. "Can I speak to you for a moment?" she asks. Oh no, not without a counselor to mediate, I think. But I say, "This is my prep period and I have a lot of errands to run, but if you make an appointment with the counselor I'll be happy to meet with you."

"This will only take a moment," she says, sitting down on the bench outside of the principal's office. I sit down too, gingerly—ready to bolt.

"I want to apologize for my behavior in your classroom," she says. I think to myself, don't say it is okay, because it was NOT okay. I just sit and listen. She continues, "I mean, what you are trying to do is really heroic. I'm sorry I gave you such a bad time."

"Yes," I smile, "what I am trying to do IS really heroic. Thank you for your apology."

*   *   *   *

A parent of one of my students is really good at making me feel that no matter what I am doing, I am not doing enough. Although her son isn't completing his work and seems disrespectful, somehow our parent conferences always seem to drift towards what I should be doing differently, rather than to what her son, Jake, should be doing differently. So today, as I walk downstairs to the counseling office to meet with her armed with my grade book, I am determined that I will be calm and professional and not let her rattle me. I enter the office and smile. "I am here to discuss Grake's Jades," I say.

*   *   *   *

Peggy looks sad and asks to speak to me as she is leaving class. "Sure," I tell her, "go sit on the couch and I'll be right there." After hall duty, I join her. "What's up?" I ask.

"I have a problem in my science class," she says. "My teacher gave a test. We were supposed to supply definitions. For the definition of 'Homo sapiens,' I put 'humankind.' He marked it wrong and didn't give me any points, and said I should have put 'mankind.'" I comfort her and ask Frank to talk to the science teacher, as I figure he will listen to Frank better than to me. Frank does, but the teacher doesn't change his policy.

The next year, when this same thing happens to Shoshannah, however, she writes a great research report on the uses of "humankind" versus "mankind," legitimizing the word, and she changes his mind at last.

* * * *

Another science teacher begins his math classes by announcing that research shows that girls don't do very well in math, so they shouldn't worry about it too much. After all, boys don't do very well in English either. When the students tell me this, I say, "Oh, right, Faulkner and Shakespeare were pretty terrible writers, I guess there's no chance for girls to do well in math or science either." I go to talk to the teacher about what he is saying. He is polite but does not change. He makes this same announcement year after year.

* * * *

One day Lia looks depressed. She is a straight "A" student. "What's wrong?" I ask.

"I just got something wrong on my science test," she says.

"What?" I ask.

"Well, the test was on class rules. It was a fill-in test. The question was, 'The legs of your chair should be on the yellow . . . blank,' and I wrote 'line.'"

"What was the answer?" I ask.

"It should have been, 'The legs of your chair should be on the yellow . . . mark.'" (This teacher has painted yellow lines—sorry, marks—on his floor so the students' desks will be lined up in neat rows.)

"Oh, Lia," I say sadly.

* * * *

Arthur, a sixth grader, has a very hard time sitting still. Every day I read to the class after lunch, and every day Arthur has to be reminded to stop drumming his pencil on the table, or to stop swinging a yoyo around, or to refrain from getting up in the middle of the story to look out the window. I am sympathetic to his need to move around, but consistent in my request that he sit and listen for fifteen minutes each day. On this day, Arthur is tapping his pencil on the table. I stop reading. "Arthur, please put your pencil away," I say. He pretends to do so. A few minutes later he is tapping away again. This time I just stop reading and wait for him to put away the pencil. He reaches under his desk for his backpack. But once under the desk, seems distracted and totally absorbed in his backpack, forgetting the rest of the class. He begins to play with something. Now, Arthur's desk is right in front of my teacher's stool, where I perch to read stories. He may think he is invisble, but I can see everything he is doing. One hand seems to be stuck in his backpack. He twists around to try to reach the other hand into his back pocket, but he can't quite make it. He goes through amazing contortions. I watch his struggles, trying to figure it out. Finally, I say calmly, "Arthur, did you accidentally handcuff yourself?"

"Yes," he says.

"Well come up here and I'll help you get loose." He turns around so I can get the keys, and I unlock the handcuffs. He returns sheepishly to his seat, and I resume my reading, but after a few minutes I burst out laughing. "Arthur, I'm not laughing at you," I say, "but that was such a great example of how hard it is for you to sit still." Arthur laughs with me. The class laughs. How many people accidentally handcuff themselves when they are supposed to be sitting quietly? A few weeks later we are walking through the Oakland Museum on our way to a special exhibit. Arthur is by my side as we walk through a section of dungeon-like weapons, including iron chains and leg irons. "I'm glad you didn't have those in your backpack," I say, and we laugh again.

*   *   *   *

My eighth grade students come in from lunch very distressed. There is a rumor going around the yard that the faculty has determined a dress code for graduation. The students are angry. I haven't heard anything about it, but it is clear that it would be foolish to put anything but this on the agenda for today's lesson. We telephone the main office and ask an administrator or counselor to come to our room to explain what is going on. "Yes," the counselor tells us, "there is a dress code that is going to be strictly enforced. No off-the-shoulder dresses, no black dresses, no strapless dresses, no gloves, no hats, no heels higher than two inches, no tuxedos—" I can't remember all the "nos."

Students are very unhappy. After they have time to talk about their feelings, they talk about what they can do. Maggie, in particular, is upset. "I already bought my dress, and it is off the shoulder," she cries. "I spent my own money on it, and I'm not sure I can exchange it, since it came from a thrift shop."

"Maybe your parents can write a letter," I suggest, but Maggie decides to talk to her counselor. She is crying.

The counselor takes her to the principal. The principal tells her to bring the dress to school the next day, to put it on, and to come to his office. He will look at it and decide if it is appropriate for graduation. The next day, Maggie brings her pink lace dress to school. She puts it on in the bathroom. She comes to my room first for moral support. I am having a very hard time, sending her off to parade in front of the principal. "Tell me everything he says," I say.

Maggie and her counselor go to the principal's office. She stands in front of his desk. "You look very pretty," he tells her. "The dress will be fine, you may wear it. Now, Maggie, don't tell anyone else that I made a special case for you. Don't tell anyone else about our talk."

"Oh," she says, "I've already promised Ms. Logan that I will tell her everything you say."

"That's all right," he says, "you may tell Ms. Logan, but don't tell other students."

When she returns to my room, she says that the principal said that if someone wears a tuxedo, he will still let him graduate off stage, but he is hoping that this rule will prevent people from doing so.

How unfair, I think. It is the person who follows the rule, then, who will be punished. I think about what we are teaching our children here: make secret deals with the principal; ignore rules instead of working together to change them. I wonder why all this energy is being expended on what students wear to graduation. I think it is a class issue. The majority of our students are students of color. Many of them are on welfare. For some of them, graduation from eighth grade is a major family celebration. They wear tuxedos and formal dresses, and they are clearly sexually mature. Others still wear slacks and shirts, or cotton dresses and flats. But the administration is very uncomfortable with this diversity. "You are not graduating as an individual," the principal says frequently, "you are graduating as a class." It is interesting to me that we belong to a school that prides itself on diversity, but we want everyone to look alike. The next year, the principal asks for and receives PTA funding to buy the eighth grade class graduation gowns. No more arguments about what to wear.

*   *   *   *

Madeline, one of my outstanding sixth graders, is leaving school a few weeks early. Her parents help run a Buddhist retreat, to which the family needs to move in May. They give me lots of advance notice, so I have some lessons for her to take with her, and she will receive full credit for the year. But I will miss her. This is my last month of school, too, since I am planning on taking a one-year sabbatical. On Madeline's last day, I ask her to stay after class a moment, and I give her a good-bye card and a glass marble for her to look at and remember us by. "I will really miss you," I say. She looks troubled, and gets a bit defensive. "I can't help it, I have to leave, my family needs to move."

"Yes, I know," I reassure her. "You have good reason to leave. It is okay for you to go. And, it is okay for me to miss you."

"Anyway," she says, with just a trace of resentment, "you are going too. You'll be gone for a whole year."

"Yes," I say. "And it is okay for me to go, too. And it is okay for you to miss me." We smile at each other.

*   *   *   *

We are in the school library, beginning our research for the quilt honoring women in American history. The librarian is looking on as I give some preliminary instructions, and the principal walks in and is also looking on.

Ruby raises her hand. "Ms. Logan, don't you think you are excluding the boys by giving yet another lesson centering on women?"

"No, Ruby, I don't," I say, and I finish my instructions. But two of Ruby's girlfriends have nodded their heads in agreement at her question, so later I take the three of them aside to talk to them. "Let's see," I say, "we did the NOW essay contest, and now we're doing the quilt. That is two lessons that center on women. This is your history we are talking about, but I take it you think I'm being excessive?"

"What about Black History Month?" Ruby says.

"We did men and women on that assignment," I reply. But the girls still seem resistant, angry. Ruby says, "I don't know, Ms. Logan, I feel that I am learning too much about women, and not enough about men, especially men of color." Her friend, Jocelyn, chimes in, "And I feel that I don't know enough about George Washington."

"Well," I reply, "Mr. Foreman and I plan your curriculum in three year segments. Some things are stressed in sixth grade, global and national things are stressed in seventh and eighth grade. You have seen my India bulletin board in class, next year when you are in seventh grade, you will be studying women and men in other countries, like India."

"Yes," they say, "but you won't be here." Hmmm. Obviously I'm not going to be able to just slip out on this sabbatical without being punished for it. "That's true," I say. "I won't be here. But someone else will be here to teach the seventh grade curriculum. And I will be back when you are eighth graders." I wonder to myself whether they will punish me in their eighth grade year, too.

The next day, I hand Ruby a stack of pictures of men of color. "Here, Ruby, you are in charge of putting these around the room." When I go to pick up a movie I have ordered for the day, I see that there is a ten minute film on George Washington. I bring it to class, and before I show it I say, "This movie is dedicated to Jocelyn." The class watches it dutifully, Jocelyn and I flash each other a look. Mine says, "See? I listen to what you say, be careful what you ask for." Hers says, "Lighten up, I get it."

kerry

SOME OF KERRY'S story I have already told, or al-
luded to. Here is the rest of what I remember. As a sixth grader, Kerry was
shy and withdrawn. She was pale, with long pale blond hair, and though
she was a talented writer, she didn't speak in class easily. Her only friend
in class was Tasha, who had serious problems. Tasha lived with her father
and her two year old sister. Her father was dying, suffering from dementia,
and was sometimes violent. I remember that she was not allowed to come
to my house for a tea party, or to attend field trips that extended past three
o'clock. She was in charge of her little sister whenever she was not in school,
and I remember her telling me that when her father ranted and raved, she
would lock herself in her bedroom with her little sister on her lap, and play
video games as loud as they would go, to keep from being scared. We had
counselors and social workers on this case, and Tasha's father died before
they could remove her from the home. She then left the school and moved
to another city in order to live with her mother. While she was at school,
however, she and Kerry ate lunch together, and took the bus to and from
school together. Except for Tasha, Kerry was a loner.

After Tasha left, Kerry bonded with my student teacher, Ellen, and wrote
in her journal one day, "Would you like to have dinner together sometime?
We could go for sushi." Kerry was lonely. In October, for our Spooky Tales
Contest, she wrote a story called "The Glass Doll and the Music Box" (see
the end of this chapter), about a girl who kills her mother and father. By
this time I was worried about her, and after talking to her counselor, we met
with her father and suggested some counseling. (Kerry had lived alone with
her father since she was seven.) We set up a session at Kaiser Permanente,
but I found out later that they didn't attend. We at least saw to it that a
counselor/intern met with Kerry regularly in school.

I spent that summer in Ireland. I returned in the Fall and gave Kerry
photographs of the Kerry Theater, the Kerry Market, the Kerry bus, and
Kerry street signs.

In the seventh grade she began to be absent frequently, and for long
stretches. We called home about it and her father said she was suffering
from cramps and headaches, but he would try to get her to school more

regularly. Her appearance began to change. She dyed her hair a flat black, she shaved part of her head, sometimes parts of her hair were purple. She had lots of earrings in one ear, and she wore only black clothes. But she had more friends, and she continued to do well in her classes.

In the eighth grade her appearance became even more extreme. It seemed that her hair changed every week. Sometimes the pale blond hair just ended in black or purple as her real hair grew out. But the more bizarre her appearance, the more I saw the pale sixth grader underneath. The day after Halloween, she came to my class looking really terrible. "What happened?" I asked. "I have been out all night long, riding the buses," she said. "I'm afraid to go home, I had a fight with my father, I'm exhausted, I'm scared." "Are you on any drugs?" I asked. "No." She really looks awful, like she could collapse. She lies down on the classroom couch, I put my coat over her, and she sleeps deeply for hours. I call my friend, Nancy, who is a health worker, and who has counseled Kerry before. "I think she is in a serious crisis," I say, and Nancy kindly agrees to come to school and to meet with her the next day. I offer to call Kerry's father for her and to mediate their meeting, but Kerry declines, and promises to go home. We talk about alternatives to riding the buses all night in case she feels she has to leave again. I make sure she knows about Huckleberry House, the refuge for teenage runaways.

The next day, Nancy meets with Kerry for some time. "She is in a crisis," Nancy says, "but she's handling it. She knows her alternatives, she is really very mature."

One day not long after this, a group of students stay in during lunch and visit together while I am puttering around. They get into a heated discussion about something or other. Later, I ask one of them, "What's up?"

"Kerry's steady boyfriend was at a party with someone else on Halloween. Kerry wasn't there. He made out with another girl at the party. Some people think that we should tell Kerry, some people think it is not our business to tell her." "Hmmm. That's a dilemma all right," I reply.

Someone does tell her, eventually, and she breaks off this steady relationship. Everyone likes Kerry, and she gets a lot of support from her many friends. Everything seems fine.

But the Monday before Thanksgiving, during homeroom, a student comes to my room to tell me that Kerry has just been found in a remote corner of the third floor in the school. She had brought a razor blade and her baby blanket to school, she had gone outside on a terrace, and she had slit her wrists. She had been taken to the principal's office, and was waiting for an ambulance. I start to tremble. This is the worst thing that can happen to a teacher, I think. No, the worst thing is if her attempt is successful. I don't have a class after homeroom, so I go tell Frank. "I will go see her," I tell him, "then I will come and cover your class so you can go see her."

When I enter the principal's office, she is huddled by the desk, her wrists are wrapped up, her counselor is there with her. I go put my hand on her shoulder, but she shrugs it off and says angrily, "This was NOT supposed to happen." "What was supposed to happen?" I ask. "I was supposed to die," she says.

"I'm glad you didn't die, Kerry," I say. "Your counselor will go with you to the hospital. I will call you later. I am going to watch Mr. Foreman's class right now so he can come see you before you go. You will be well taken care of."

As I walk to Frank's class, I meet students from our GATE program in the hall, scared and horrified at what has happened. The news is traveling fast. When Frank returns from seeing Kerry, we agree to call Suicide Prevention and get counselors into the school immediately. But before we do, I go upstairs to see my friend Suzanne (our AV clerk), who was the person that found Kerry and took her razor blade away. Suzanne lost her younger sister to suicide, so I know this must be a particularly bad experience for her. I give her a hug, I thank her for what she did, I tell her that Kerry is on her way to the hospital, that the counselor will stay with her and make sure she gets admitted for treatment. "I was glad I could help save her," Suzanne says, and her mouth is trembling. I wonder if my mouth is trembling, too.

I call my friend Nancy, who comes to school immediately and helps me make phone calls. Suicide Prevention agrees to send counselors to meet with the seventh and eighth grade classes in the afternoon. I call McAteer High School, and they agree to send students from their peer counseling center immediately. Students are clustering in my classroom, crying, holding on to each other, talking. "Kerry is going to be okay," I reassure them, "but what has happened is really terrible—it is okay to be scared, sad, whatever." By noon, Margo has arrived from Suicide Prevention. We decide to put two classes together for sixth and seventh period. Nancy will meet with one group, Margo with the other one. We want to send a letter home to parents, telling them what happened so that they can talk to their children and help them cope, but the administration doesn't think it's a good idea. (Two days later, however, they give their approval and we send a letter home with the students.)

Margo goes around her group and has everyone tell how she or he is feeling. There is a lot of guilt, anger, fear, sorrow: "If only I had known, I could have done something." "I said something mean to her last week, could that have made her do this?" "I just feel really afraid." "What if she were really dead now?" We talk about how suicide is a permanent solution to a temporary problem. We talk about how to get help if someone threatens suicide.

Margo meets with the teachers, too. "You are doing the right thing," she says, "just let them keep talking about their feelings. Watch for students who are isolating. Suicide attempts affect everyone involved, and people in the school are at risk for at least six months—teachers included—even students from other programs who did not know Kerry. We can expect other suicide gestures, we should be on the alert for signs, we should take all symptoms seriously." It feels like the aftermath from a major earthquake: we are under stress, preparing for possible aftershocks.

On the outside, I am calm and professional. On the inside I am like a fierce tiger. I cannot do anything for Kerry right now—she has been admitted to a hospital for psychiatric treatment for at least a month—but I can be alert and watchful so that this doesn't happen to any of the others. I know that suicide gestures in teenagers can spread like a bad rash. I am terrified that someone else will try this and succeed. At night, when I go to bed, I mentally go over the day, checking to see if there was any behavior that I should be noticing. The tiger in me prowls and paces, ever watchful.

We arrange for a Suicide Prevention counselor to address the faculty, so all teachers can get information on what to watch for, on what to do. We arrange for an evening parent meeting so that Margo can help parents deal with their feelings, and so that she can educate them about suicide. We encourage all students to talk to their parents. We arrange for the peer counselors to be in my classroom for the next two days. If only I can make it until Thanksgiving, I think, I will have four days to rest and recover.

The first suicide gesture comes just one day after Kerry's attempt, on the Tuesday before Thanksgiving. The counseling office calls me. "We have Matt in the office," they say. "We have taken a razor blade away from him. He has cut himself up and down his arms. Although he is not your student, he says he won't speak to anyone but you and Frank."

I get Frank and we go to the office. On the way, I think about Matt. I don't really know him well—I know he is friends with a lot of my students, especially Kerry, and he comes into my room to visit sometimes, but I have never had him as a student. He is a slight, quick, thin child with a stray puppy look.

When I get to the office he is sitting in a chair looking at the floor. "Let me see your arms," I ask, and he pushes up his sleeves. My heart breaks when I see the thirty or so superficial slashes on his arms. What is this about? I ask myself, Why did he want to see you and Frank?

I lean down so my eyes are even with his. "Matt, did you do this so we would send you to the hospital with Kerry, so that you can be with her?"

He starts to cry. "Yes," he says. "She needs to be with her friends. She shouldn't be all alone."

"She isn't all alone," I say, "she is in good hands, and people will take good care of her." I look at the counselor. "I think we should call the hospital and let him talk to her," I say. "He needs to hear that she is okay." She nods and dials the phone. Frank and I stay with him until Matt's mother arrives to take him to a therapist.

Parents call me and they, too, are upset. Johannes' mother arranges to take a whole carload of kids down to the hospital to see Kerry. "I know it's too soon for them to visit with her," she says, "but they need to see her, even if it's just down the hall. I need to see her," she says. She starts to cry. "This is so sad. When she gets out, she could come to our house and stay with us," she says.

It feels like I am always on the phone. When I am not on the phone, the fierce tiger in me is prowling around, observing student behavior. If a child lingers at the pencil sharpener too long, I begin a mental file on him—is he isolating? We finally make it to Thanksgiving.

On the day before Christmas vacation, on a crowded streetcar as we return from taking Too Many Kids to see *A Christmas Carol*, Frank tells me, "Frankie says that James is talking about suicide. We better take him into school and talk to him when we get back." James? He is one of our best students. He has a great family. His mother is a professor, his father has a catering business. Both parents come to all school meetings. Both parents are clearly involved with and concerned about their children's lives. Why would James be thinking of suicide? But we take him up to my room when we get back to school. It is four or five o'clock and everyone else goes home.

"Are you thinking of committing suicide, James?"

"Yes."

"Have you thought about how you would do it?"

"No."

"Have you thought about when you would do it?"

"No." (Good, he's not in immediate crisis.) "I don't want you to tell anyone about this," he says.

"Why are you thinking about it?" we ask.

"I'm just not getting along with my parents," he says vaguely. "I like Frankie, but she doesn't like me."

Frank talks to him about adolescent problems, about suicide being a permanent solution to a temporary problem, about talking to his parents. We negotiate a contract with him. He will not do anything without calling us first. When he leaves, we talk about this, but neither of us can figure out why he is suddenly in crisis.

It is the evening of the first day of Christmas vacation, but I am awake, tossing and turning: *Something is wrong, something is wrong, something is wrong. If I go over everything carefully enough, there is a clue somewhere as to what is really wrong with James.* I think about it all day Saturday, as I go about my life, but I remain deeply puzzled. *Something just doesn't make sense.* I toss and turn: *What is it? What is it?* Finally, about four in the morning, I sit up in bed. My brain finally offers up some information. It was James who told Kerry that her boyfriend had been making out with someone else at the Halloween party. I also remember that James was not in school Thanksgiving week—he was home with the flu. He missed all of the counseling sessions. As soon as I have figured this out, I can finally go to sleep.

The next morning I call James' home early. His mother answers the phone. "There is a serious problem I would like to come and talk to you about," I say.

"Good," she says, "I wish someone would come and tell me what's going on. Our phone is ringing off the hook with James' friends, and he won't talk to us."

"I'll be right over," I say.

When I get there, she makes coffee, and James and his mother and father and I sit around the kitchen table. I have asked him to join us so he can hear everything I say. "I know you asked me not to talk about this," I tell him, "but this is too serious for me to keep to myself." I tell his parents about his suicide threat, about Kerry's history, and about how I finally figured out the connection between his story and Kerry's story. "He needs counseling right away," I say. His mother is very supportive. His father is polite but defensive, and I don't blame him. Here I am in his home on a Sunday morning describing a serious problem. If Frank and I were so surprised, imagine how James' parents must feel. When I finish my story, I look at James. He seems more relieved than angry at me, he says that everything I have said is true, he feels responsible for Kerry's suicide attempt. His parents promise to get immediate help, and I take my leave.

A big voice inside of me says, *Take care of yourself. Go get some breakfast. Go home and go to bed.* I take a bath, as I have that sticky film all over that comes with emotional stress. That night, James' father calls me. "I want to thank you for coming over this morning," he says. "We had a long talk with James after you left. But, he was wrong. He shouldn't have told Kerry anything about her boyfriend. I think he understands that."

"I don't think this is about making a judgment," I say. "This is about giving him some love and support. He is feeling guilty and vulnerable, he doesn't need us to tell him he was wrong." When our conversation ends, and I have hung up the phone, I let out a good scream. It feels good, so I let out another one. I call Nancy. "I seem to be screaming," I say, "do you think I might be going crazy? "

"What are you screaming about?" she asks. I tell her. "No, you're not crazy," she says, "it sounds pretty healthy to me."

James' mother calls a few days later, also to thank me, and to tell me that James has begun therapy, and that both she and his father will participate in this therapy too. "It was really brave of you to come and see us," she says.

The next suicide gesture comes some weeks later. Patricia is talking to her friend Maggie on the phone. "I have just taken half a bottle of pills," she tells Maggie, who lives across the bay.

"Just a minute, my mom is on the other line," Maggie says. She puts Patricia on hold and dials 911, giving them Patricia's address. (I'm not the only fierce tiger on the prowl.) She gets back on the line and continues the conversation. Soon Patricia hears the ambulance sirens, but the ambulance cannot find her house, so Maggie hangs up and calls James' mother, who lives quite close to Patricia. James' mother goes to Patricia's house immediately and takes her to the emergency room. Right before having her stomach pumped, Patricia admits that while she took half the bottle of pills, there were only two pills in the bottle, so she actually took only one pill. They keep her for observation and send her home; we follow up at school and get her into therapy. "I wanted to see what Maggie would do," Patricia says in therapy. "I wanted to see if she was really my friend."

Sarah starts coming into my room more and more often during lunch. She sits by herself. She seems depressed. I have a long talk with her mother. She begins counseling.

Meanwhile, we have had the faculty meeting and the parent meeting on suicide prevention. I seem to be forever on the phone. Soon Kerry will be released from the hospital. The school administration wants her to transfer to another school. We are five months away from graduation, but they want her to start all over at another school. Frank and I dig in our heels: "No. She has been here for two and a half years. All her friends are here, and she needs her friends. She has a good rapport with her teachers. The rest of the students need to see her returning to school and a normal life. If she disappears there will be no closure here." The school agrees to consider keeping her, but we need to arrange for a big deal summit meeting that includes Kerry, her father, her therapist, her father's therapist, the supervising psychiatrist, a counselor representing the district, the school counselor, the principal, Nancy, Margo, Frank and me. It takes a long time, but after much discussion and reassurances that Kerry has adequate support, we win. After another period of intense counseling while she is living at home, she will be allowed to return to school and graduate with her class. We agree to have Margo and the peer counselors at school the week she returns, in order to help everyone adjust.

The next suicide gesture comes in writing. A student describes in her journal about two attempts she has made. This also surprises me, because she is such a good student, she seems so well adjusted. But when we talk, I uncover some serious stress in the family, and some emotional abuse, so we work with her and her family until they, too, are safely in therapy.

Before Kerry returns to school, Margo speaks to each class about the importance of staying true to one's feelings. "If you didn't like her before, you don't have to like her now," she says. "If you are her friend, just continue with normal life. You can talk to her about anything you want."

"What if she does it again?" someone asks.

"We have a pretty good support system set up here," Margo explains. "But, ultimately, nobody can prevent someone else from committing suicide if they really want to. Remember everything you have learned so far—

tell an adult if you see any of the signs, in Kerry or in anybody else. But if something happens, it is not your fault."

On the day Kerry comes back to school, we arrange for her to begin the day in Frank's art class. Margo is there, I am there, and a peer counselor from McAteer High School is there, in case anybody needs to talk about how they are feeling. We have sort of an overkill support system set up. But Kerry comes in as though nothing has happened, and the students all seem comfortable and natural, so I just visit with the other counselors. Most of the students have already seen and visited with Kerry outside the school setting, so they are not seeing her for the first time.

I am nervous when Kerry first comes in, as I know that she is nervous. I don't stare or anything but I take care to observe how she is doing. When she goes to get her art portfolio, as she joins a group and starts chatting with others, I feel like a person whose unreliable car has just started up.

The next weeks and months continue in a relatively normal manner. We still, however, keep close tabs on our five suicide gestures, we keep watch for others, we continue our support for other students, but things seem smoothed out.

In June, Frank and I sit in the balcony of the auditorium and watch the eighth graders march across the stage to get their diplomas. It is our tradition to sneak the seventh graders into the balcony to watch their friends graduate, even though the bulletin says not to bring students. Every year the principal sees us up there, but he never says anything. I am always teary at graduation, but this year I am more so. As the last student walks across the stage and the school band gets ready to play, I turn to Frank and say, "Well, they're all alive."

THE GLASS DOLL AND THE MUSIC BOX
by Kerry

It was a small blue-grey music box. The inside was lined with black felt. In the center was a glass doll; a dancer. It was clear glass with a painted face, hair, tutu and point shoes. She stood in fifth position, arms extended, bowing slightly. She stood on a spring and turned when the box was wound. The music it made was a faint, fabricated, eerie, rhythmical, ringing. This is its story.

In the year 1904, a girl lived with her mother and father. She was very shy and mostly kept to herself. It was probably because of her parents. They were very strict. She didn't like her parents but was very afraid of them. A friend of her mother's had recently died and they went to the cemetery. Her parents told her to wait by the entrance. A while after her parents had left she noticed something poking out of the ground. It was a small blue-grey music box. She scratched away the dirt and pulled it up. When her parents came she hid it behind her back. Her parents talked to each other the whole way home so they did not notice or ask about the music box. The girl went immediately up to her room and placed it on her end table. When she went to bed she opened it, wound it and went to bed.

The box began to play its slow eerie tune as the dancer turned slowly and the girl dropped off to sleep. It took up to a month or more before it started to happen. But slowly, slowly, it began to take effect. The girl would lie in bed, the music would play and it seemed to her that the music came from somewhere deep inside her head and not from the music box at all. It seemed like it was going out rather than coming in.

The song began to pound in her head. She felt nervous, angry, frightened, and a mix of emotions. Run, scream, cry, laugh, anything, and then she would fall asleep. It became worse. Her head hurt worse now and it hurt all the time. She never said anything and she kept winding the box every night, even when she didn't want to. It was like a drug; she couldn't stop. Then one night while she lay in bed and the box played, the pounding and the aching seemed to come from her whole body. In the pain her eardrums burst and blood dripped from her ears.

She sat up and in her horror saw that the expression on the doll had changed to an evil grin. As if a puppet controlled by strings, she got up from the bed and broke a piece of her mirror. She walked to her parents' room and walked in. She slit her mother's throat before she had a chance to scream, and pushed the piece of glass into her father's chest and left the room. She went back to her room and laid down. She was found the next morning, said to have died of a heart atack. The house was cleaned and the music box was placed in the attic.

Eighty years later the family that lived in the same house was cleaning out the attic. They also had a daughter. In the corner she found a blue-grey music box. She took it to her room. At bedtime she put the box on her dresser top, wound it and opened it. The box began to play its slow, eerie tune as the dancer turned slowly and the girl dropped off to sleep . . .

notes on teacher-centered resource time

TODAY MY NEXT door neighbor—who is the principal of what is considered to be one of the "toughest" middle schools in San Francisco (read "poor and African American")—told me about a job. She mentioned that she had a full-time resource teacher position available at her school.

I was tempted to apply, because I am tired.

But I don't believe in resource teachers. Or, I should say, I don't believe in the THEORY BEHIND resource teachers, since I know a lot of terrific resource teachers personally. As many of us know, resource teachers spend five periods a day helping classroom teachers by teaching model lessons in their classes, finding books and materials they might need, helping them to come up with strategies for individual students or particular lessons, and feeding them ideas.

But I believe that the heart of the educational process is in the daily classroom connection that is woven between a teacher and the students. Education is not something that you can separate from this day-to-day process. Education builds on itself, and the hundreds of insights that a teacher gains from this daily process is the warp through which the threads of education must be woven. No matter how dynamic a particular lesson is, it remains only a particular lesson if it tries to exist outside the context of the daily classroom continuum.

I have seen great teachers leave the classroom to become resource teachers. To me, this is like taking a great parent, a mother, for example, and separating her from her children so that she can travel from family to family in order to model good parenting, or to cook for them, or to read the bedtime story, or to choose the elementary school for the younger children. THERE IS NO WAY THAT THIS CAN WORK. Yes, she can be a help from time to time, yes, she might even make some children think, "I wish my mother were like her," but by cutting herself off from her own family, she has done more damage than she can possibly repair by being of help to others.

By separating themselves from the daily experience of being a classroom teacher, resource teachers lose touch with the powerful unexpectedness of the daily opportunities to validate growth that have nothing to do with materials, techniques, or frameworks. This ongoing PROCESS between teacher and student is the heart of education, and I have never seen a resource teacher, no matter how talented, brilliant, or dedicated she or he may be, who has not eventually "lost heart."

To know this makes me somewhat sad, because I am tired. I do not want to "lose heart" by leaving the classroom, but I don't want to die of a heart attack from the stresses and strains of classroom teaching, either.

The root of the problem here is that the classroom teacher is frequently seen as being at the bottom of a hierarchical pyramid. To be offered a job as a resource teacher, or an Access teacher, is to be offered a "step up." Many people seem to think that you can only gain prestige and power once you stop teaching in the classroom. But I don't see it that way. I think that in disconnecting myself from daily contact with a particular group of students I not only marginalize myself in an unacceptable way, I also cut myself off from the joy of the educational process that can occur only in a long, given stretch of time.

My suggestion, then, in order to "keep heart" and to avoid heart attacks, is to eliminate the position of resource teacher, and to take those periods of time given to the resource teacher (five or six a day) and distribute them to the individual classroom teachers. Each classroom teacher would then become her or his own resource person, and the resource person would in turn become a classroom teacher. Instead of teaching five classes a day with thirty-two to thirty-six students in each class, the classroom teacher would teach four classes and have one period to collect his/her own materials, ideas, and strategies. This would diminish the idea of an "expert" helping those who are seen as "not expert"—which is in itself somewhat divisive and hierarchical—while also eliminating the extra time needed for the resource teacher to communicate with the classroom teacher, since the resource teacher WOULD BE the classroom teacher.

Also, this plan would address the overworked, exhausted state of the classroom teacher. Being given one period in which to catch one's breath and have the energy and enthusiasm for planning lessons—instead of trying to cram it in at the end of an exhausting, stressful day—would do wonders. But this won't fix everything, because the hierarchical, unspoken assumption that the classroom teacher is somehow on the bottom rung of the educational ladder—and thus an inferior teacher—leads to the assumption that pullout programs and resourcing will somehow help make things better. We are trying to patch that which we ourselves have damaged by not acknowledging the importance of the daily classroom experience.

For example, because of the disastrous state of our educational budget in the state of California, I worry about a trend towards making even more programs—such as GATE and Special Ed—pullout programs, further disrupting the continuity of the classroom. As a result of such a trend, the classroom teacher has different students pulled out to get diagnosed and taught by someone else, leaving her with a different population of students in the classroom every day. Continuity and long range planning becomes difficult. Or, an "expert" teacher comes into the classroom to do a dynamite lesson on, say, descriptive writing. If this lesson is really terrific, and it usually is, it makes the students sad that this doesn't happen every day, and it leaves the teacher demoralized because she or he doesn't have the time and resources to create that kind of dynamite production on a daily basis.

Another problem is that the resource teacher often comes in with a whole different set of student expectations from the classroom teacher. (Raise your hand before you speak/don't raise your hand before you speak; don't interrupt each other/speak your mind out loud and clear; sit on the floor and make yourself comfortable in the classroom/sit up straight at your desk at all times; "compete, compete"/"cooperate, cooperate.") The classroom teacher then either has to back up a whole set of rules and expectations that she doesn't agree with, or she has to be willing to pit herself against the resource teacher, who is supposed to be there to help her.

One of the arguments for having a resource teacher is that he or she is given an amount of time—say, one day a week and/or parts of each day—to familiarize herself with lots of materials, ideas, strategies, techniques, etc. She then has a real smorgasbord to offer the classroom teacher that the classroom teacher does not have time to prepare herself, given her lack of time and energy for such things. But I see a serious drawback in this method of resourcing others. First of all, the resource teacher begins to think of materials in isolation from students and the process of learning. Any classroom teacher knows that an idea that worked at ten o'clock on Friday doesn't necessarily work at eleven o'clock on Friday, or that materials that worked really well last year just might bomb out this year. The process of education is a dynamic one that has a mysterious element to it; it cannot be reduced to charts of skills or lists of books or even to frameworks of ideas. True, it is all of these things, but it is also *much* more. So the resource teacher's understanding, and thus effectiveness, is diminished by not becoming involved with this mystery, and often tends to overemphasize the tools of education, losing touch with the process.

And the classroom teacher's effectiveness is diminished by not being honored with the time to work out her own creative solutions to the unique problems of her classroom. To remedy this problem, I think ten classroom teachers could be given one resource period a day, as well as time each week to share ideas and materials with others teaching in their field, for every two full-time resource teachers in a school. This would keep good teachers in direct relationships with students, and would also provide opportunities to share teaching insights with other teachers.

Many years ago—twelve or fifteen—I proposed this idea at my own school. I was put on a committee for a year to study all the possibilities. We did so, and gave a thorough report on the advantages of classroom teachers being their own resource teachers. But this plan is more difficult for administrators to manage. We were told that the plan was not feasible because of funding: the resource teachers were paid from federal funds, the classroom teachers were paid from city funds. It was too complicated to try to get five twenty-percent paychecks from the government instead of one full-time one. So much for a year on a committee.

Another argument for having a resource teacher is that since not all teachers are good ones, students stuck with a bad teacher will at least get one good lesson from the resource teacher every week or two. But I see it differently. If that great resource teacher were in the classroom, students would be getting a dynamic education every day, not just every week. Although education pretends to be the great equalizer, we have always had some teachers who are better than other ones; but the solution here is not to siphon off the good ones (to "reward them" by taking them out of the classroom), but to empower and inspire the not so good ones. It is of interest to me that in my twenty-five years of observing teaching, most pressure by administrators seems to be brought on outstanding teachers, not on mediocre ones.

Another problem in this hierarchical view of things is that resource teachers can be seen by classroom teachers as "tools of the administration." And they can be perceived by administrators as people who can get classroom teachers to "stay in line," therefore cutting down on the administrator's need to communicate with faculty. Resource teachers can easily get caught in between the two, especially when administrators reluctant to deal directly with teacher ideas or teacher problems can be tempted to use the resource teachers as buffers. However, if every teacher in the school were four-fifths classroom teacher and one-fifth resource teacher, these divisions would disappear, and better communication would take place all around.

more notes

LAURA BURGESS IS an observer in my classroom, preparing for her student teaching assignment. She tells me about a curriculum class she is taking at San Francisco State University in which they read a choral poem about American history. "Every chorus started with the line, 'Now there was a man!'" Laura says. (It was a very Phase One poem.) Laura decides to write a play for her curriculum class project. She does weeks and weeks of research, and writes *American Women Making History*. She turns this project in, gets an "A," and generates a wonderful discussion about gender inclusive curriculum among these future teachers.

Laura leaves us to begin student teaching in an elementary school. The students and I miss her, and we decide to perform her play and present it to her as a surprise, because although she has written it and read it and discussed it, she has never SEEN it.

We work hard learning the play. We create a big mural background that says "AMERICAN WOMEN MAKING HISTORY, By Laura Burgess." We gather hats and shawls for costumes. When we are finally ready, I invite Laura to our school for lunch. We buy a big bouquet of flowers and set it in the middle of the room on the floor, sort of creating a stage area. We invite the principal and another sixth grade class to be our audience, but Laura has the chair of honor. We have a wonderful time performing Laura's play for her. She has created a piece full of women heroes, and it is amazing to me to watch my male students happily performing female roles. They don't mind being female when females are presented as valid, strong, important people. After the play we cry, "Author! Author!" and we give her the flowers.

This event is such a success that I begin to think about what to do next.

I call KALW, our local community radio station, and they send someone over to hear our play. He likes it, and schedules us to be on the radio for Women's History Month. The students are really excited about this project. They practice hard and do a professional job. Laura and I are interviewed after the performance. I make a mental note about taking our work out into the community more often.

I introduce Laura to the women from the National Women's History Project in Santa Rosa, and they publish her play and put it in their catalogue. (She has received royalties ever since.)

The next year I arrange for my students to design a bookstore window display for Women's History Month. We have to do this after school, and one year only boys volunteer for this assignment. I love watching them choose which materials to display, which student work to highlight, how to best arrange things to catch the eye of the public. We leave a blank notebook next to the display so that people can write their comments about our display. (We end up doing this for several years.)

*   *   *   *

It is more than twenty years ago. I am a new teacher teaching in a junior high in the Hunter's Point/Bayview district of San Francisco. Ninety-four percent of the student body is African American, and more than half of the students live in public housing. The curriculum guide tells me that I am to teach *Lamb's Tales from Shakespeare* to my eighth grade classes.

Ooohhh, they're going to hate this, I think. So I find a quote by Bertrand Russell that says that school ruins Shakespeare for kids. If they could only meet him in the flesh, he says, full of jollity and ale. I climb on my teacher's stool and share the quote. "How does school ruin things you love?" I ask. I get a lot of examples. We have a great discussion. "Well, school sometimes does that to Shakespeare too," I say, "which is really a shame because he wrote a lot of interesting stuff." I tell them a little about Shakespeare's life, about his passion for plays. "Shakespeare found stories in lots of places and turned them into plays," I explain. "Lamb took Shakespeare's plays and turned them back into stories. We are going to take these stories and turn them back into plays, just as Shakespeare did. Find a partner or a group to work with. You don't have to read all of Shakespeare's stories, but choose one that you want to turn into a play. At the end of this assignment we will have a Shakespeare Festival and you will each present your play."

I am amazed at how this catches on. "Can we make posters to advertise our play?" Yes. "Can we put them up around the room?" Yes. "Can we bring stuff in for costumes and props?" Yes. "We are shy. We don't want to do a play in front of the class. Can we put ours on the tape recorder and just do a radio play?" Yes. "Can we do ours with puppets?" Yes. "We're having trouble figuring out how Shakespeare would have handled this scene . . . can we look at his script to see how he did it?" Well, yes (!) "Our play takes place in Verona (or Troy, or Dunsinane, or Denmark), can we make a map to show where that is?" Yes. Students from my remedial reading classes notice these posters and maps appearing in the room. "Can we do that too?" Sure.

The librarian from the Third Street Library calls me. "What have you done? All the books on Shakespeare are checked out of the library for the first time ever."

When it is time for our festival, I am delighted with what the students have done. They come up with a marvelous mix of Shakespeare juxtaposed with Hunter's Point (read "Harlem," if you are unfamiliar with San Francisco). In *Julius Caesar*, for example, a student dressed in a white sheet, waving a cardboard sword, bellows "Friends, Romans, Countrymen, lend me your ears and I'll lower your taxes!"

Two students from *Romeo and Juliet* circle nose to nose and shoulder to shoulder. "You phony old Capulet," one says. "You jive ass Montague," the other one replies, "your mother." It is not Laurence Olivier, but they have the general idea. Students do a whole range of plays. After this festival we talk about what they have seen. ("What have you learned about Shakespeare?" "He wrote a lot about many different things, about different times and different places. He's fun.") We learn about tragedies and comedies and history plays. When some agency offers our school free tickets to go see *Henry IV,* Part One, all my students sign up.

At least I haven't done any damage, I think. We've survived the curriculum guide.

*　　　*　　　*　　　*

I am a new teacher and I have entered a school where the culture is almost totally unfamiliar to me. I am the only white person in the room. The curriculum guide says I am supposed to teach dictionary skills. "Pretend you are a person coming to the projects from New York," I say to the class. "You will be taking the bus to school, walking the halls, going to class, spending time on the playground. What are the words and phrases you might hear that would be unfamiliar to you but that you would need to understand in order to survive?" Students begin to list words and phrases like "shining you on." ("That's like, you know, you're sitting on the bus looking out the window and you see your friend walking on the street but you pretend you don't." "Or you're eating something good and your friend asks for some and you just act like you didn't hear him. That's shining him on.") Or: "That's tight. That means, like, stingy, or selfish, or cruel."

They sometimes give me more than one definition or example. We alphabetize this dictionary and number the definitions. We use this class dictionary as a prelude to our "real" dictionary lesson, and I, who am not from New York at all but from San Francisco, begin to learn about the culture of my students.

*　　　*　　　*　　　*

I am standing in front of this same class and we are supposed to be reading about Tom Sawyer, and I am explaining how Samuel Clemens changed his name to Mark Twain, but I am feeling terribly irrelevant to these children's lives. So I bring in some music that was popular during the sixties: "Oh Happy Day." Close your eyes and listen to this music and tell me what makes you happy, I say. We create a class poem on the board about happiness. I feel better.

*   *   *   *

Another memory of my first classroom: I take pictures of each class and have them blown up into posters and put them up around the room. The classroom finally reflects us. I put their classwork up on the bulletin boards next to their class poster.

*   *   *   *

It is the sixties and cities are rioting. One of our school's former students is killed in Hunter's Point. This child was a passenger in a stolen car, and was shot and killed as he fled the scene after police stopped the car. His body is left in a field for some hours before it is taken away, and some of our students see the dead boy on their way home from school. This was the incident that triggered the San Francisco riot.

In school the students write about what is happening. I discover that they all think the National Guard was called out to protect them from the police. I learn a lot. Students begin to write plays about the Black Panthers, with characters like Bobby Seale, Huey Newton, Angela Davis and Eldridge Cleaver. They fight over who gets to play each part.

Students come to school with axes, pokers, and knives. "I am glad you came to class," I say, "but leave all the weapons in the corner by the door."

I am teaching in this school when Martin Luther King is assassinated. We spend the day talking, crying and writing haiku:

Black and White together
He struggled for all of us
Martin Luther King

We make a memorial booklet.

A few months later Bobby Kennedy is in California campaigning for the Presidency. I have a mock election in my class, and I am shocked when Bobby Kennedy loses. "Why is this?" I ask, "I know you really like Bobby Kennedy—he visited the projects here just weeks ago, he is very popular. How did he lose this election?"

"If we vote him in they will just kill him," the students say. This happens in all of my classes. I am shocked and saddened. I give my talks about hope, faith, and that just because it happened to Martin Luther King and John Kennedy doesn't mean it will happen to everyone you care about.

I come home and talk about this at the dinner table. "What can I do to turn this around?" I say to my husband, and I go to bed early, depressed and exhausted. Later, he comes in and shakes my shoulder.

"Honey, wake up, Bobby Kennedy has just been shot." "That's not funny," I say, and roll over. "Get up," he says, "I'm not kidding." I am up for hours, hoping Kennedy will live, and I return to school the next day and face my students. They are kind and do not say "I told you so."

*   *   *   *

I am a beginning teacher and this class gives me a running account every day of how I'm doing. "You doing good, teacher, but wait 'til Donald Lance gets here, then you're in trouble." "Those boots are nice, teacher, you doing just fine today, but wait 'til Donald Lance gets here." "The boys just like you 'cause you got a big butt, teacher, but I like you 'cause you're nice. I hope you do okay with Donald." "Teacher, did you make that dress yourself? You put that zipper in by hand? Nice. Are you pregnant?"

Each day I take attendance and each day Donald Lance is absent and each day the class warns me about him when I take roll. One day a very mature young man walks into class. He is probably only fifteen, but he seems to be about twenty-five. (I am twenty-four.) He exudes rage. The class settles down to watch. I have never seen them so attentive. The student who must be Donald Lance walks to the back of the room and stands at the window.

"Class," I say, "please take your seats" (although everyone is seated except the new student). "I cannot start class until everyone is seated." Pause. Donald continues to stare out the window. Finally, I say, "Donald, please sit down." And his rage explodes. He climbs on a chair and puts one foot on the attached table, he gives me the finger with both hands, and he starts yelling, "Fuck you, teacher, fuck you up your ass!!" The class watches me carefully. I have adrenalin coming out of my ears. This child looks as though he would like to kill me, and could. I remember that at the new-teacher meeting on discipline, the dean said that we should send referrals down to the office with the student if at times something happened that we could not handle. This seems like one of those times. "Do not put generalities on the referral," the dean said, "be specific."

So while Donald continues to yell and give me two fingers, I reach in my desk drawer for referrals and as calmly as possible I write, "When told to take his seat, Donald climbed on it and yelled, 'Fuck you, teacher, fuck you up your ass.'" I fill out the homeroom, date, and time, and hold it out in my hand. I am trembling all over and the paper shakes. I am not a brave person. "Donald," I say, "please take this referral downstairs." And to my surprise, HE DOES! I never see him again.

"You did good, teacher," the class tells me, but this incident never leaves me, and twenty-five years later I still worry about it.

*   *   *   *

I stayed at that school for five years. Everything I really needed to know about teaching I learned there. But each year I lost at least one student to a violent death—stabbings at parties, car accidents, shootings. The politics of the school and the community drained energy from good teaching. Finally, I was offered a job at another middle school and I decided to transfer. My students gave me a farewell party, and said, "You going to a tough neighborhood, teacher, those Mission kids are TOUGH, you better be careful."

Years later Kay, a fellow teacher, asks me to take one of her special ed students into my classroom for one period a day. "He is really smart," Kay tells me, "and he would benefit a lot from your class discussions and projects." So I take Austin into class, and sure enough, he really is smart, but while he is great during discussions, he rarely does any work. Kay invites me to the next parent conference where I meet Austin's mother, who has several small children with her. She keeps looking at me. Finally she says, "Did you used to teach at Mission High School?" "No," I say, "but I taught at Bayview." "Yes," she says, "Ms. Logan," and we look at each other for a few moments as we begin to recognize each other. She is a former student, I am her former teacher. I feel some anxiety as I watch her assessing me. We are both remembering what Bayview was like. It was where I learned about institutional racism. The students referred to it as "The Jailhouse."

Austin's mother looks at me and says quietly, "You did the best you could."

*   *   *   *

One day I came home and announced to my friend, Claudia, that I had finished my book. "That's wonderful, Judy," she said. "Congratulations!" Then, after a pause she asked, "How do you know you're finished?"

"Because it is the middle of June," I tell her. "All teachers know that if it's the middle of June we must be finished."

*   *   *   *

selected bibliography

Bloom, Benjamin. *Taxonomy of Education Objectives, Handbook I: Cognitive Domain.* New York: David McKay Pulishing Company, 1956.

Eustis, Helen. "A Lickin' a Boy Could Be Proud of," from *A Family is a Way of Feeling.* New York: The Macmillan Company, 1966.

Forbes, Kathryn. "Mama and Her Bank Account," from *Mama's Bank Account.* New York: Harcourt, Brace, and World, 1943.

Hughes, Langston. "Thank You, Ma'am," from *A Family is a Way of Feeling.* New York: The Macmillan Company, 1966.

McIntosh, Peggy. "Interactive Phases of Curricular Re-Vision: a Feminist Perspective, Working Paper No. 124" (1983), and "Interactive Phases of Curricular and Personal Re-Vision with Regard to Race" (1990). Wellesley, MA: Center for Research on Women, Wellesley College, Wellesley, MA 02181

Morgan, Carol McAfee. "Anita's Gift" from *A Family is a Way of Feeling.* New York: The Macmillan Company, 1966.

Rogers, Lilith. "For Angela at Puberty," from *Lilith Returns.* Sebastopol, CA: Green Snake Press, P.O. Box 2455, 1989.

Rush, Anne Kent. *Moon, Moon.* New York, NY and Berkeley, CA: Random House and Moon Books, 1976.

Saroyan, William. "The Parsley Garden," from *Counterpoint in Literature.* Sacramento, CA: California State Series, 1967.

Style, Emily. "Curriculum as Window and Mirror," from *Listening for All Voices: Gender Balancing the School Curriculum.* New Jersey: Oak Knoll School Monograph, Summit, 1988.

Tavris, Carol and Baumgartner, Dr. Annette I. "How Would Your Life Be Different?" *Redbook*, 1983.

Taylor, T. Roger. *Building a Quality Program for Gifted Students Resource Handbook.* Paso Robles, CA: Bureau of Education and Research, 1989.

Wright, Richard. "The Streets of Memphis," from *Coping.* New York: The Macmillan Company, 1966.

Order Form for *Teaching Stories*

❖

NAME _____

ADDRESS _____

CITY _____

STATE _____ ZIP_____

HOME PH. _____

WORK PH. _____

❖

Please note that larger orders are discounted.

Orders of 19 or fewer:

_____ (# of copies) @ $11.95 ea. = _____

Orders of 20 or more:

_____ (# of copies) @ $7.00 ea. = _____

(Minnesota residents add 6-1/2%
sales tax or tax exempt number) = _____

Shipping and handling = _____
(10% of total cost; $2.00 minimum)

Total enclosed = _____

MAIL TO:
Minnesota Inclusiveness Program
1125 Harbor Lane North
Plymouth, MN 55447

OR FAX: 612–473–9350